READING
EXPLORER

THIRD EDITION

2

PAUL MACINTYRE

DAVID BOHLKE

**NATIONAL
GEOGRAPHIC**
L E A R N I N G

Australia · Brazil · Mexico · Singapore · United Kingdom · United States

NATIONAL GEOGRAPHIC
L E A R N I N G

National Geographic Learning,
a Cengage Company

Reading Explorer 2
Third Edition

Paul MacIntyre and David Bohlke

Publisher: Andrew Robinson

Executive Editor: Sean Bermingham

Senior Development Editor: Christopher Street

Director of Global Marketing: Ian Martin

Heads of Regional Marketing:

Charlotte Ellis (Europe, Middle East and Africa)

Kiel Hamm (Asia)

Irina Pereyra (Latin America)

Product Marketing Manager: Tracy Bailie

Senior Production Controller: Tan Jin Hock

Associate Media Researcher: Jeffrey Millies

Art Director: Brenda Carmichael

Operations Support: Hayley Chwazik-Gee

Manufacturing Planner: Mary Beth Hennebury

Composition: MPS North America LLC

Student Book with Online Workbook:
ISBN-13: 978-0-357-12470-3

Student Book:
ISBN-13: 978-0-357-11626-5

National Geographic Learning
20 Channel Center Street
Boston, MA 02210
USA

Locate your local office at **international.cengage.com/region**

Visit National Geographic Learning online at **ELTNGL.com**
Visit our corporate website at **www.cengage.com**

Printed in China
Print Number: 01 Print Year: 2019

CONTENTS

SCOPE
AND SEQUENCE

ACADEMIC SKILLS

READING SKILL	VOCABULARY BUILDING	CRITICAL THINKING
A: Skimming for the Main Idea of Paragraphs B: Identifying the Purpose of Paragraphs	A: Phrasal verbs with *cut* B: Collocations for size adjectives	A: Applying Ideas B: Evaluating Items
A: Understanding Pronoun Reference B: Scanning for Details	A: Prefix *inter-* B: Suffix *-tion*	A: Identifying Reasons B: Applying Concepts; Synthesizing Information
A: Creating a Timeline of Events B: Distinguishing Facts from Speculation	A: Words acting as nouns and verbs (1) B: Collocations with *cruel*	A: Justifying Opinions B: Evaluating Evidence
A: Dealing with Unfamiliar Vocabulary (1)—Using Context B: Differentiating Between Main Ideas and Supporting Details	A: Prefix *pro-* B: Prefix *en-*	A: Applying Ideas B: Relating Information; Applying Ideas
A: Interpreting Infographics B: Dealing with Unfamiliar Vocabulary (2)—Affixes	A: Words acting as nouns and verbs (2) B: Collocations with *access*	A: Analyzing Claims B: Ranking Items
A: Understanding Cause-and-Effect Relationships B: Recognizing Contrastive Relationships	A: Collocations with *negative* B: Prefix *in-*	A: Evaluating Ideas B: Analyzing Reasons; Evaluating Sources
A: Summarizing Using a Venn Diagram B: Recognizing and Understanding Synonyms	A: Suffix *-able* B: Collocations with *distinctive*	B: Applying Ideas; Evaluating Pros and Cons
A: Taking Notes on a Reading (1) B: Taking Notes on a Reading (2)—Using a Concept Map	A: Word forms of *admire* and *observe* B: Prefix *mis-*	A: Inferring Information B: Applying Ideas; Evaluating Arguments
A: Understanding Claims B: Making Inferences	A: Phrasal verbs with *go* B: Collocations with *severe*	A: Reflecting B: Justifying Opinions; Reflecting
A: Identifying Supporting Information B: Identifying Arguments For and Against an Issue	A: Collocations with *shift* B: Phrasal verbs with *up*	A: Evaluating Claims B: Analyzing Arguments; Inferring Information
A: Dealing with Unfamiliar Vocabulary (3)—Using a Dictionary B: Understanding a Research Summary	A: Collocations with *average* B: Word forms of *honest*	B: Evaluating a Claim; Applying Ideas
A: Understanding Definitions in a Text B: Taking Notes on a Reading (3)—Creating a Visual Summary	A: Synonyms for *fantastic* B: Collocations with *out of*	A: Ranking Activities B: Synthesizing Information

READING EXPLORER brings the world to your classroom.

With *Reading Explorer* you learn about real people and places, experience the world, and explore topics that matter.

What you'll see in the Third Edition:

Real-world stories give you a better understanding of the world and your place in it.

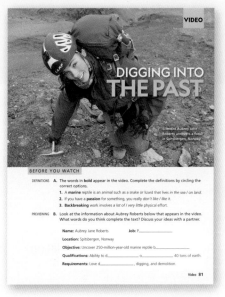

National Geographic Videos
expand on the unit topic and give you a chance to apply your language skills.

Reading Skill and **Reading Comprehension** sections provide the tools you need to become an effective reader.

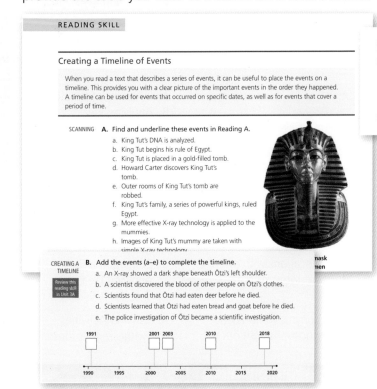

CRITICAL THINKING Evaluating a Claim

▸ Ariely says, "Cheating is easier when we can justify our behavior." Look at the situations below. How might each person justify their behavior? Discuss your ideas with a partner.

1. A soccer player pretends to be injured even though he is fine.
2. A worker takes home some office stationery to use at home.
3. A salesperson sells a product that he knows isn't very good.

▸ List some other examples of common dishonest behavior. For each example, do you think the behavior can be justified? Discuss with a partner.

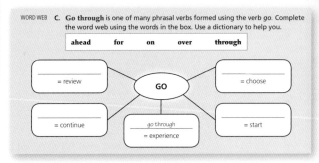

Expanded Vocabulary Practice sections teach you the most useful words and phrases needed for academic reading.

FOOD AND HEALTH

A group of friends enjoy a traditional meal in Cappadocia, Turkey.

WARM UP

Discuss these questions with a partner.

1. What are some healthy foods you like? What unhealthy foods do you enjoy?

2. Do you think the foods people eat today are healthier than those in the past?

It's not surprising that a cupcake contains a lot of sugar. But what about other foods?

BEFORE YOU READ

QUIZ **A.** How much sugar do you think is in these foods? Match the items below. Check your answers at the bottom of page 10.

1. 100 g of low-fat fruit yogurt • • a. 3 grams

2. 2 small chocolate cookies • • b. 7 grams

3. 100 g of tomato ketchup • • c. 11 grams

4. 1 cupcake with frosting • • d. 15 grams

5. 2 slices of wheat bread • • e. 25 grams

SCANNING **B.** Why do you think people love sugar so much? Discuss with a partner. Then scan the first paragraph of the reading to check your ideas.

SWEET **LOVE**

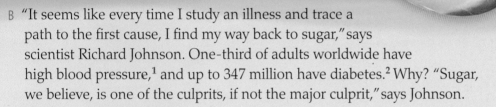

A Many scientists believe our love of sugar may actually be an **addiction**. When we eat or drink sugary foods, the sugar enters our blood and affects the parts of our brain that make us feel good. Then the good feeling goes away, leaving us wanting more. All tasty foods do this, but sugar has a particularly strong effect. In this way, it is in fact an addictive **drug**, one that doctors **recommend** we all **cut down on**.

B "It seems like every time I study an illness and trace a path to the first cause, I find my way back to sugar," says scientist Richard Johnson. One-third of adults worldwide have high blood pressure,[1] and up to 347 million have diabetes.[2] Why? "Sugar, we believe, is one of the culprits, if not the major culprit," says Johnson.

C Our bodies are designed to survive on very little sugar. Early humans often had very little food, so our bodies learned to be very **efficient** in **storing** sugar as fat. In this way, we had energy stored for when there was no food. But today, most people have more than enough. So the very thing that once saved us may now be killing us.

D So what is the solution? It's **obvious** that we need to eat less sugar. The trouble is, in today's world, it's extremely difficult to avoid. From breakfast cereals to after-dinner desserts, our foods are increasingly filled with it. Some manufacturers even use sugar to replace taste in foods that are **advertised** as low in fat. So while the foods appear to be healthier, large amounts of sugar are often added.

E But some people are fighting back against sugar and trying to create a healthier environment. Many schools are replacing sugary desserts with healthier options, like fruit. Other schools are trying to encourage exercise by building **facilities** like walking tracks so students and others in the community can exercise. The **battle** has not yet been lost.

---

1 If you have **high blood pressure**, your heart needs to work harder to pump blood around your body.
2 **Diabetes** is a medical condition in which someone has too much sugar in his or her blood.

A. Choose the best answer for each question.

GIST **1.** What is the reading mainly about?

   a. our addiction to sugar
   b. illnesses caused by sugar
   c. ways to avoid sugar

VOCABULARY **2.** In paragraph B, the word *culprit* is closest in meaning to _____.

   a. disease
   b. sweet food
   c. cause of the problem

REFERENCE **3.** In paragraph C, what does the phrase *the very thing* refer to?

   a. the amount of sugar in our food
   b. having enough food to survive
   c. our ability to store sugar as fat

DETAIL **4.** According to the passage, why is it so hard to avoid sugar?

   a. It gives us needed energy.
   b. It's in so many foods and drinks.
   c. We get used to eating it at school.

DETAIL **5.** Which of the following statements about sugar is NOT true?

   a. Our bodies are able to store sugar as fat.
   b. We need very little sugar to survive.
   c. Early humans ate more sugar than we do today.

△ **Macarons are colorful sugary cookies.**

SCANNING **B.** Write short answers to the questions below. Use one to three words from the passage for each answer.

1. What disease do a third of adults in the world suffer from?

_____

2. Why do some manufacturers add sugar to low-fat foods?

_____

3. What are many schools replacing sugary desserts with?

_____

Answers to Before You Read A:
1. 11 g, 2. 7 g, 3. 15 g, 4. 25 g, 5. 3 g

∨ **Even fresh fruits like strawberries contain small amounts of sugar.**

Skimming for the Main Idea of Paragraphs

Skimming a text can help you quickly understand its main ideas. When you skim, you don't read every word. Instead, read the first sentence of each paragraph, and then run your eyes quickly over the rest, focusing on the main nouns and verbs. If you understand the main idea of each paragraph, you will have a good understanding of the passage as a whole.

DETERMINING MAIN IDEAS

A. Look back at Reading A. Circle the main idea of each paragraph A–C.

1. **Paragraph A**
   a. Sugar is addictive.
   b. All tasty foods contain sugar.

2. **Paragraph B**
   a. Sugar can cause illnesses.
   b. The number of people with diabetes and high blood pressure is rising.

3. **Paragraph C**
   a. Sugar gives us energy when we don't eat for a long time.
   b. Our bodies need very little sugar to survive, and we now eat too much of it.

DETERMINING MAIN IDEAS

B. Complete the sentences to summarize the main ideas of paragraphs D and E.

1. **Paragraph D:** These days, it is very difficult to _____.

2. **Paragraph E:** There are some people who _____.

CRITICAL THINKING Applying Ideas

▶ In the space below, list some foods and drinks that you regularly consume.

tacos, pasta, cookies, salad, diet soda, burritos, oatmeal, chicken, rice.

▶ Look back at your list. If you want to reduce your intake of sugar, which of these items should you cut down on? If necessary, research online to find out how much sugar is in each item.

COMPLETION **A.** Complete the information using the correct form of the words in the box. Two words are extra.

> **addiction   battle   drug   recommend   store**

The story of sugar began in New Guinea about 10,000 years ago. People there picked sugarcane and ate it raw. Because it made people feel good, they saw it as a(n) [1] _drug_ that could cure illnesses. Doctors in India [2] _recommend_ that people eat it to stop headaches. But soon people began to eat it for pleasure. Demand for sugar rose as people started to develop a(n) [3] _addiction_ to the taste. By 1900, it was recorded that the average British person ate 45 kilograms of sugar each year.

DEFINITIONS **B.** Complete the sentences. Circle the correct options.

1. When a company **advertises** something, they want you to *buy / return* it.
2. Someone who is **efficient** at a task does it without *planning carefully / wasting time or energy*.
3. Two groups that have a **battle** are likely to be *angry at / friendly with* each other.
4. The **facilities** of a school include the *classrooms / teachers*.
5. If something is **obvious**, it is *difficult / easy* to see or understand.
6. When you **store** something, you *keep it / throw it away*.
7. When you **cut down on** sugar, you eat *less / more* of it.

▲ A market seller in Myanmar makes fresh sugarcane juice.

WORD PARTS **C. Cut down on** is one of many phrasal verbs formed using the verb *cut*. Complete the definitions below using the correct preposition in the box. One preposition is extra.

> **across   in   off   up**

1. If you cut _off_ a supply of something, you stop providing it.
2. If you cut something _up_, you cut it into many pieces.
3. If you cut _in_ while someone is talking, you interrupt them.

BEFORE YOU READ

MATCHING **A.** Look at the photo and read the caption. Match each word in **bold** with its definition.

1. found   a. to keep safe for future use
2. preserve   b. to start an organization
3. species   c. type (usually of plant or animal)

PREDICTING **B.** Why do you think people like Cary Fowler want to protect certain plant species? Discuss your ideas with a partner. Then skim the passage to check your ideas.

⌄ **Conservationist Cary Fowler holds two containers of peas outside the Svalbard Global Seed Vault, Norway. Fowler founded the vault in 2008 with the aim of preserving various species of plants.**

FOOD
FOR THE FUTURE

A   In 1845, a deadly disease struck the farms of Ireland, killing all the Lumper potato plants. The death of a single **crop** species might not seem so important. But in Ireland, in 1845, people depended almost solely on the potato for food. The death of one species caused a terrible famine.[1] Now, some scientists are worried that such a famine could happen again—but on a much wider **scale**.

B   Over the centuries, farmers have discovered thousands of different species of food crops. Each species has special **qualities**. Some can be grown in very hot or cold climates. Others are not affected by certain diseases. However, you won't find many of these species in your local supermarket. To feed the seven billion people on Earth, most farmers today are growing only species of plants that are easy to **produce** in large numbers. Meanwhile, thousands of other species are becoming extinct.[2]

C   For example, in the Philippines, there were once thousands of **varieties** of rice; now fewer than 100 are grown there. In China, 90 percent of the wheat varieties grown just a century ago have disappeared. Experts believe that over the past century, we have allowed more than half of the world's food varieties to disappear.

Saving the Seeds

D   One solution to this problem is to collect and preserve the **seeds** of as many different plant varieties as we can before they disappear. This idea was first **suggested** by Russian scientist Nikolay Vavilov. In the 1920s and 1930s, he collected around 400,000 seeds from five **continents**. More recently, others have continued the work he began. There are now around 1,700 seed banks in countries around the world. The Svalbard Global Seed Vault—which preserves almost one million seed samples—has one of the largest collections.

E   In the U.S. state of Iowa, Diane Ott Whealy and her husband founded Heritage Farm—a place where people can store and trade seeds. Initially, Ott Whealy wanted to preserve **historic** plant varieties, like the seeds her great-grandfather brought to the United States more than 100 years ago from Germany. But the people at Heritage Farm don't just store the seeds; they plant them. By doing this, they are reintroducing foods into the marketplace that haven't been grown for years. These food species are not just special in terms of appearance or **flavor**. They also offer farmers food solutions for the future, from the past.

---

1   A **famine** is a situation in which large numbers of people have little or no food.

2   If a species becomes **extinct**, it no longer exists.

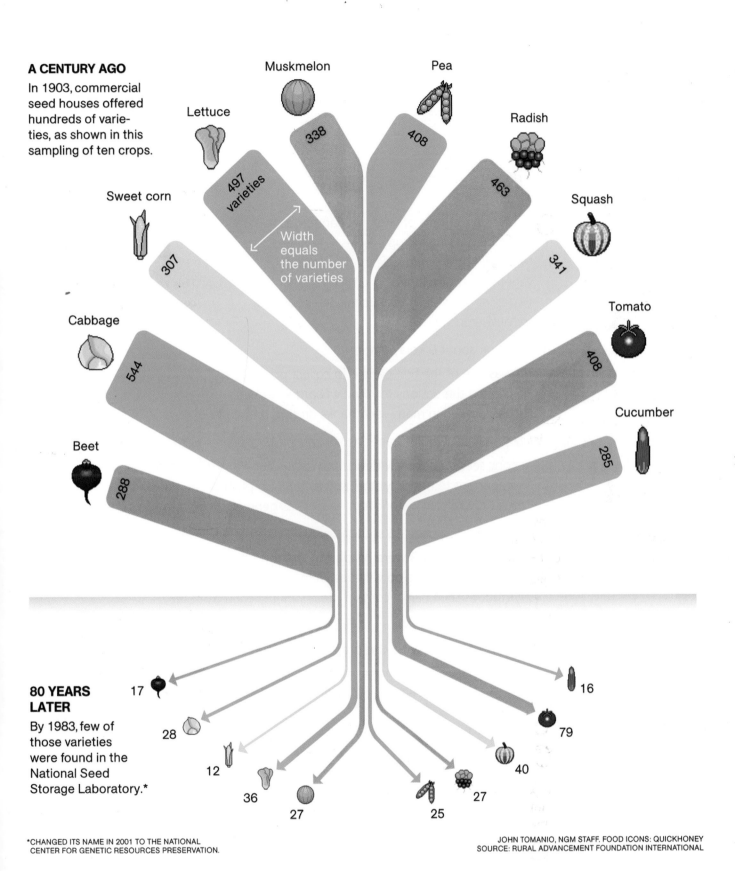

A CENTURY AGO

In 1903, commercial seed houses offered hundreds of varieties, as shown in this sampling of ten crops.

Muskmelon

Pea

Lettuce

Radish

Sweet corn

Squash

Cabbage

Tomato

Beet

Cucumber

497 varieties

Width equals the number of varieties

338

408

463

307

341

544

408

288

285

80 YEARS LATER

By 1983, few of those varieties were found in the National Seed Storage Laboratory.*

17

16

28

79

12

40

36

27

27

25

*CHANGED ITS NAME IN 2001 TO THE NATIONAL CENTER FOR GENETIC RESOURCES PRESERVATION.

JOHN TOMANIO, NGM STAFF. FOOD ICONS: QUICKHONEY
SOURCE: RURAL ADVANCEMENT FOUNDATION INTERNATIONAL

A. Choose the best answer for each question.

GIST

1. What is the reading mainly about?

   a. how food species disappear
   b. the need to preserve different food species
   c. ways to increase the number of food species

PURPOSE

2. Why does the writer mention Ireland in the first paragraph?

   a. to give an example of why it is dangerous to depend on a single crop species
   b. to explain how worldwide interest in crop varieties first developed
   c. to describe how Irish researchers are searching for new crop varieties

∧ **This rare variety of wild corn now exists only in seed banks.**

DETAIL

3. What is true about Nikolay Vavilov?

   a. He was one of the first people to collect plant seeds.
   b. He created the designs for the Svalbard Seed Vault.
   c. He has worked in many seed banks around the world.

INFERENCE

4. Which statement would Diane Ott Whealy probably agree with?

   a. Historic seeds are usually difficult to reintroduce to the marketplace.
   b. It's important to not only store seeds, but also plant them.
   c. Foods grown from historic and new seeds generally have a similar taste.

INFERENCE

5. The infographic on page 15 shows _____.

   a. that farmers in 1903 were producing less food than farmers today
   b. that many different crop varieties were lost between 1903 and 1983
   c. that today's seed banks contain more varieties than those in 1903

MATCHING

B. Match each statement with the place it describes.

| a. China   b. Iowa, U.S.A.   c. Ireland   d. the Philippines   e. Svalbard |

1. _b_ Historic plant varieties are being planted and sold here.

2. _c_ Many people died here because of a serious lack of food.

3. _a_ Only 10 percent of past wheat varieties now remain here.

4. _d_ There are now far fewer varieties of rice here than in the past.

5. _e_ One of the biggest seed banks in the world can be found here.

Identifying the Purpose of Paragraphs

Different paragraphs may perform different functions. Identifying their purpose can help you better understand the organization of a text. Some paragraphs may have more than one function. Common purposes include:

- to provide background information
- to introduce a topic
- to present an argument
- to offer or describe a solution
- to offer another side of an issue

- to describe a situation or problem
- to report data as figures or statistics
- to summarize key ideas
- to provide examples or explanations
- to present a conclusion

IDENTIFYING PURPOSE

A. Look back at Reading B. Choose the correct purpose of each paragraph.

1. **Paragraph A**
   (a.) to provide some historical background
   b. to summarize the key ideas

2. **Paragraph B**
   a. to offer another side of the issue
   (b.) to describe a situation or problem

3. **Paragraph C**
   a. to summarize some key ideas
   (b.) to report data as supporting evidence

4. **Paragraph D**
   a. to present a conclusion
   (b.) to offer or describe a solution

5. **Paragraph E**
   (a.) to present an argument
   (b.) to provide an additional example

∧ **As well as seeds, some farmers are working to preserve species of farm animals, such as this rare variety of chicken.**

IDENTIFYING PURPOSE

B. Now look back at Reading A. Note the purpose of each paragraph.

1. Paragraph A: Introduce a topic/describe a problem
2. Paragraph B: Report data/stadistics
3. Paragraph C: Provide background info
4. Paragraph D: Describe the problem
5. Paragraph E: _____

COMPLETION   **A.**   **Complete the information. Circle the correct words.**

Over 1,700 seed banks around the world keep seed ¹(**varieties**)/ **flavors** from all ²(**qualities**)/(**continents**) safe in the event of a large-³(**scale**)/ **produced** global crisis, such as a famine. The Svalbard Global Seed Vault is one of the world's largest. Director Cary Fowler commented that the opening of the seed bank "marks a ⁴**seed** /(**historic**) turning point in safeguarding the world's ⁵(**crop**)/ **flavor** diversity." The seeds are stored in a permanently chilled, earthquake-free zone 120 meters above sea level, allowing them to remain high and dry.

∧ **Cary Fowler inside the Svalbard Global Seed Vault on Spitsbergen island**

DEFINITIONS   **B.**   **Match each word in red with its definition.**

1. _j_ **crop**
2. _g_ **scale**
3. _h_ **seed**
4. _f_ **produce**
5. _b_ **flavor**
6. _e_ **variety**
7. _c_ **suggest**
8. _d_ **historic**
9. _i_ **continent**
10. _a_ **qualities**

a. features or characteristics
b. how something tastes
c. to put forward an idea
d. important to the past
e. a range of different types
f. to make or create
g. the size or extent of something
h. part of a plant from which a new plant grows
i. land consisting of countries (e.g., Asia)
j. a plant grown in large amounts, like wheat

COLLOCATIONS   **C.**   **The adjectives in the box are used with certain nouns to mean "big" or "large." Complete the sentences using the words in the box.**

high	strong	wide

1. Buffets often have a ___wide___ **variety** of dishes that you can try.
2. This coffee has a rather ___strong___ **flavor**.
3. The restaurant offers a range of ___high___-**quality** vegetarian options.

18 Unit 1B

^ Astronauts have a pizza party on board the International Space Station.

SPACE
FOOD

BEFORE YOU WATCH

PREVIEWING **A.** Read the information. The words and phrases in **bold** appear in the video. Complete the definitions by circling the correct options.

In 1962, astronaut John Glenn became the first man to eat anything in the **zero gravity** environment of Earth orbit. He found the task of eating fairly easy, but wasn't so impressed with the menu—apple sauce packed in a tube, sugar tablets, and water. The food eaten by astronauts has improved a lot since these early days of space travel. Modern astronauts stay in space for longer **durations**, so a tasty and **balanced diet** is essential.

1. If you have a **balanced diet**, you eat *many* / *very few* different types of food.
2. The **duration** of something is how *heavy it is* / *long it lasts*.
3. In **zero gravity**, objects *do not fall* / *fall* to the ground.

PREDICTING **B.** What do you think are the most important things to consider when creating food for astronauts? Discuss with a partner and note your ideas.

Space food needs to be …

Easy to eat
Easy to prepare
Healty

GIST **A.** Watch the video. Which of your ideas in Before You Watch B are mentioned?

SHORT ANSWER **B.** Watch the video again. Note answers to the questions.

1. What are two benefits of freeze-dried food?

_____Is ligther_____

2. How often do astronauts make their own food while in space?

_____Rarely_____

3. What was the reason for the pizza party?

_____

CRITICAL THINKING Evaluating Items   Look at the list of food items below and consider what you learned about space food in the video. Rate the items 1–5 (5 = great space food; 1 = terrible space food). Share the reasons for your choices with a partner.

____ breakfast cereal   ____ dried fruit   ____ potato chips

____ cheese   ____ instant noodles   ____ sashimi

____ chicken legs   ____ nuts   ____ soup

VOCABULARY REVIEW

Do you remember the meanings of these words? Check (✓) the ones you know. Look back at the unit and review any words you're not sure of.

Reading A

☐ addiction   ☐ advertise   ☐ battle   ☐ cut down on   ☐ drug

☐ efficient   ☐ facilities*   ☐ obvious*   ☐ recommend   ☐ store

Reading B

☐ continent   ☐ crop   ☐ flavor   ☐ historic   ☐ produce

☐ quality   ☐ scale   ☐ seed   ☐ suggest   ☐ variety

* Academic Word List

CALL OF THE WILD

Discuss these questions with a partner.

1. Why do you think the wolf in the photo is howling?

2. What are some other ways that animals communicate with each other?

> A female tundra wolf in the Alaska Wildlife Conservation Center, United States

BEFORE YOU READ

QUIZ **A.** The whale in the photo is a humpback. Humpbacks are found in most of the world's oceans. What do you know about them?

1. Humpback whales *often / rarely* swim close to land.

2. Humpbacks usually eat *small fish / penguins*.

3. Humpback whales communicate by *making sounds / moving their flippers*.

SCANNING **B.** Now scan the first paragraph of the reading to check your answers. Then read the entire passage.

A humpback whale breaches at sunrise off the coast of Petersburg, Alaska.

SONG OF THE HUMPBACK

A Herman Melville, the writer of the famous whale story *Moby Dick,* once wrote that humpback whales were "the most lighthearted[1] of all the whales." A favorite of whale watchers everywhere, they often swim in ocean areas close to land and are active at the surface. They can often be seen breaching, or rising out of the water, and then coming down with a great splash. Humpbacks are intelligent animals, and can be seen working together to hunt schools of small fish. And, if you listen closely, you might even hear one singing.

Recording Gentle Giants

B Marine biologist[2] Jim Darling has studied the songs of humpback whales for more than 25 years. While **recording** whale songs on a boat near Hawaii, he invited author Douglas Chadwick to **experience** diving with a humpback. In the water, Chadwick heard the whale's songs in a way he had never heard them before. "Suddenly, I no longer heard the whale's voice in my ears," he said. "I felt it inside my head and bones."

1 Someone or something that is **lighthearted** is cheerful and happy.
2 A **marine biologist** is a scientist who studies ocean life.

∧ A humpback whale calf. Young humpbacks do not stop growing until they are ten years old.

C   When swimming with the whale, Chadwick could see that it was **aware** of him, but not worried by his presence. The 13-meter-long giant looked him over[3] **curiously,** but never harmed him. The whale then swam under the boat. It pointed its head down to the ocean floor and, with flippers[4] extended out to its sides, began to sing. Up in the boat, Darling recorded the whale's song. Humpback whale songs can be long and **complex,** sometimes lasting for 30 minutes or more. They are perhaps the longest songs sung by any animal.

Why Do They Sing?

D   Darling says that only male humpbacks sing, but for **unknown** reasons. One idea is that they sing to attract females. However, when a group of scientists played recordings of whale songs in the ocean, female whales did not respond. Another idea is that male humpbacks use their songs to let other males know they are in the area.

E   Researchers have also found that humpback whale songs are different in different parts of the world, perhaps like whale national anthems.[5] They may also be like hit tunes on the radio, changing over time— from one year to the next, or even over a **single** breeding **season.**

F   There is still so much the scientists don't know, and years of study lie ahead for whale researchers like Jim Darling. "Why do I do it?" he wonders aloud. "Human beings like puzzles. I want to know."

G   Another member of the research team, photographer Flip Nicklin, recalls a special moment he had while **interacting** with a humpback. While he was snorkeling some distance from the huge animal, it approached him until it was just a few meters away. It then gently carried Nicklin toward its eye with a flipper, as if examining him. **Apparently,** the desire to understand a different species goes both ways.

---

3 If you **look** something **over,** you examine it for a short period of time.
4 **Flippers** are the two flat body parts that stick out from the side of a whale, seal, etc.
5 A **national anthem** is a country's song, chosen to represent its people.

A. Choose the best answer for each question.

GIST

1. What is the reading mainly about?

    a. how humpbacks communicate with people
    b. research into how and why humpbacks sing
    c. the career of a man who is interested in humpbacks

DETAIL

2. When the scientists played whale songs in the ocean, ___.

    a. no female whales came
    b. male whales became angry
    c. male and female whales sang together

DETAIL

3. What is NOT true about humpback whales?

    a. Their songs are short and simple.
    b. Only male humpback whales sing.
    c. Their songs differ from place to place.

DETAIL

4. The passage compares humpback songs to *hit tunes on the radio* because ___.

    a. the whales' songs are beautiful
    b. the whales sing songs very often
    c. the whales change their songs often

VOCABULARY

5. In the last paragraph, what does *goes both ways* mean?

    a. moves in many directions
    b. is similar for both
    c. increases quickly in size

▽ **The tail of each humpback has a different shape and pattern. Researchers use these differences to identify the whales they study.**

IDENTIFYING PURPOSE

Review this reading skill in Unit 1B

B. Match each paragraph with its purpose.

1. Paragraph C

2. Paragraph D

3. Paragraph E

4. Paragraph F

a. to describe something researchers do not know about humpbacks

b. to explain a difference between humpbacks from different places

c. to tell the personal story of a humpback researcher

d. to give a reason why researchers continue to study humpbacks

Understanding Pronoun Reference

A pronoun usually, but not always, refers to something earlier in the sentence or in a previous sentence. In the example below, the subject of the second sentence *(they)* refers to a noun in the first sentence *(humpback whales)*.

> *Herman Melville … wrote that humpback whales were "the most lighthearted of all the whales." A favorite of whale watchers everywhere, <u>they</u> swim in ocean areas …*

The context should help you understand what the pronoun is referring to.

REFERENCE **A.** What does each <u>underlined</u> word refer to? Circle a, b, or c.

1. Humpbacks are intelligent animals, and can be seen working together to hunt schools of small fish. And, if you listen closely, you might even hear <u>one</u> singing. *[handwritten: Singular]*

   (a. a humpback whale)   b. a group of intelligent animals   c. a school of small fish

2. Marine biologist Jim Darling has studied the songs of humpback whales for more than 25 years. While recording whale songs on a boat near Hawaii, <u>he</u> invited author Douglas Chadwick to experience diving with a humpback.

   (a. Jim Darling)   b. Douglas Chadwick   c. the author

3. Humpback whale songs can be long and complex, sometimes lasting for 30 minutes or more. <u>They</u> are perhaps the longest songs sung by any animal.

   a. the researchers   **(b. humpback songs)**   c. male humpbacks

REFERENCE **B.** What does each **pronoun** from the reading refer to?

1. I felt **it** inside my head and bones. (paragraph B)   *whale's voice*

2. The 13-meter-long giant looked **him** over … (paragraph C)   *Chadwick*

3. **It** pointed its head down … (paragraph C)   *The whale*

4. **It** then gently carried Nicklin … (paragraph G)   *a humback*

CRITICAL THINKING Identifying Reasons

Discuss the questions with a partner and note your ideas.

▶ What possible reasons does the author give for the humpback whales' singing?

1 To atract females
2 For males to alert males they are in the area

▶ What other possible reasons can you think of?

Peasure
Communicate with other whales

COMPLETION   **A. Complete the sentences using the words in the box. One word is extra.**

> apparently   aware   experience (n)   interact   record   single

1. Whales generally come up to breathe every 15 minutes, but some can hold their breath for up to an hour on a(n) _Single_ dive.
2. Some people are not _aware_ that many of the whales they see on whale-watching tours are later killed in areas where whaling is still allowed.
3. _apparently_, there are some whale species that do not seem to migrate at all. They spend the entire year in one place.
4. Many of those who have swum with whales have described the _experience_ as life-changing.
5. Scientists who study whales use special technology to _record_ the sounds they make underwater.

DEFINITIONS   **B. Read the information. Then complete the definitions using the words in red.**

Like humpbacks, blue whales sing **complex** songs. And like humpbacks, they are endangered. Fortunately, there are now laws that protect them. Today, although their exact number is **unknown**, the blue whale population is growing. Scientists are **curious** to know more about blue whale behavior, so they have placed cameras on them. Through these cameras, it is possible to watch the whales as they swim, eat, and **interact** with each other. Scientists have discovered that during breeding **season**, the females migrate to food-rich areas to have their babies.

1. If something is _complex_, it has many parts and is difficult to understand.
2. A(n) _season_ refers to a particular period of time during the year.
3. If something is _unknown_, you have no information about it.
4. When people or animals _interact_, they spend time together and communicate.
5. Someone who is _curious_ about something wants to learn or know more about it.

WORD PARTS   **C. The prefix _inter-_ means "between" or "together," as in the word _interact_. Complete the sentences using the words in the box.**

> action   national   view

1. She was offered an **inter**_view_ for a job as a member of a whale research team.
2. Saving endangered whales is going to require **inter**_national_ cooperation.
3. Many studies focus on the **inter**_action_ between male and female humpbacks.

BEFORE YOU READ

PREVIEWING

A. Read the paragraph below. What is special about the great horned owl and the lyrebird?

Many species of birds communicate using different calls. The great horned owl, for example, can make a great variety of sounds, each with a different purpose. Other birds are able to mimic sounds they hear. The lyrebird, for example, is not only able to copy the calls of other birds, but also to reproduce man-made noises like car alarms and chainsaws.

SKIMMING

Review this reading skill in Unit 1A

B. Skim the reading passage. Answer the questions.

What bird is the passage about? _Sparrows_

What is special about this bird's call? _The song hasn't changed for hundreds of years_

A great horned owl

THE 1,000-YEAR BIRD SONG

A swamp sparrow in Delaware, United States, sings its traditional song.

A Every summer, the calls of thousands of swamp sparrows can be heard across North America's wetlands. These little brown birds know only a few songs, but they know them very well. In fact, their musical set list[1] probably hasn't changed much for centuries.

B Like **humans**, baby swamp sparrows learn to communicate by copying adults. From a young age, they learn to copy, or mimic, songs sung by their elders. "Swamp sparrows very rarely make mistakes when they learn their songs," says biologist Robert Lachlan. In fact, their mimicry is so **accurate** that the music changes little between generations.

C Just like children, the sparrows don't remember every song they hear, Lachlan says. "They don't just learn songs at random; they pick up commoner songs rather than rarer songs." In other words, they learn songs they hear most often. It's an example of a strategy that scientists call *conformist bias*.[2] Until recently, this learning ability was thought to be special only to humans.

D Between 2008 and 2009, Lachlan's research team recorded the calls of 615 male swamp sparrows across the northeastern United States. The researchers used computer software to break each song into a collection of notes, or syllables. They then measured the differences between the tunes.

E The research revealed that only 2 percent of male sparrows sung a different song from the **standard** tune. The **combination** of accurate mimicry and conformist bias allows the birds to **create** traditions that last for centuries. "With those two ingredients together, you end up with traditions that are really stable," says Lachlan. "The song-types that you hear in the marshes[3] of North America today may well have been there 1,000 years ago."

F Lachlan's study is among the first to measure the longevity of song traditions within a bird species. Another **aspect** scientists are now exploring is the **impact** of habitat loss on songbirds. Man-made barriers—such as cities, roads, and plantations—can break up a bird population into a number of isolated groups. These barriers may prevent **cultural** interaction between songbird populations, such as the **exchange** of song types.

G The findings are really exciting, says scientist Andrew Farnsworth. He hopes that future research will **evolve** from these studies. For example, scientists may be able to identify how other animals are able to preserve their cultural traditions. "Seeing the potential for it in other organisms[4] is super cool," says Farnsworth.

---

1 A **set list** is the list of songs a musician will play during a performance.
2 **Conformist bias** is the way humans or animals tend to follow common behavior.
3 **Marshes** are wet, muddy areas of land.
4 **Organisms** are animals or plants, especially ones that are very small.

READING COMPREHENSION

A. Choose the best answer for each question.

GIST **1.** What would be the best alternative title for the passage?
- a. The Amazing Lifespan of Swamp Sparrows
- b. How Swamp Sparrows Evolved in North America
- c. The Swamp Sparrows' Traditional Set List

VOCABULARY **2.** In paragraph B, the word *elders* means ___.
- a. older swamp sparrows
- b. adult humans
- c. birds of another species

DETAIL **3.** In Lachlan's study, about how many swamp sparrows did NOT sing traditional songs?
- a. 12
- b. 600
- c. 615

Swamp sparrows can be identified by their brown wings, gray faces, and a dark line close to the eye.

INFERENCE **4.** Hundreds of years ago, the songs of swamp sparrows were probably ___.
- a. completely different from today's songs
- b. slightly different from today's songs
- c. exactly the same as today's songs

INFERENCE **5.** Which of the following is an example of *conformist bias*?
- a. A student memorizes dates for a history exam.
- b. A pet learns to do a trick because its owner rewards it regularly.
- c. A new slang word becomes popular with a group of teenagers.

EVALUATING STATEMENTS **B.** Are the following statements true or false according to the reading passage, or is the information not given? Circle **T** (true), **F** (false), or **NG** (not given).

1. Swamp sparrows learn to sing when they are young.   T F NG

2. Conformist bias was only recently noticed in animals.   T F NG

3. The swamp sparrow research was carried out all over the United States.   T F NG

4. Each sparrow song consists of more than ten notes, or syllables.   T F NG

5. Scientists are studying how habitat loss might affect bird songs.   T F NG

32 Unit 2B

Scanning for Details

Scanning a text can help you to quickly find specific information, such as a name, a date, a place, a number, or a reason. Decide what exactly you need to look for, and then quickly look only for that information. Do not read every word.

SCANNING

A. Read the questions below. For each question, decide what information you need to look for. Then scan Reading B quickly to find the answers.

1. Where do swamp sparrows live?

(name / place / date / number / reason) **Answer:** _North America wetlands_

2. Who are the two scientists mentioned in the passage?

(name / place / date / number / reason) **Answer:** _Lachoin / Farnsworth_

3. When did the research team carry out the swamp sparrow study?

(name / place / date / number / reason) **Answer:** _2008/2009_

4. How many male swamp sparrows were recorded?

(name / place / date / number / reason) **Answer:** _615_

5. Why did the researchers use computer software?

(name / place / date / number / reason) **Answer:** _To break the song into separate notes_

SCANNING

B. Scan the reading passage again and underline each piece of information below. Note the paragraph in which the information appears.

1. examples of man-made barriers — paragraph _F_
2. the main findings of the swamp sparrow study — paragraph _E_
3. an example of future research that may evolve from the study — paragraph _G_
4. how both children and swamp sparrows learn to communicate — paragraph _B_

CRITICAL THINKING Applying Concepts   Look again at the definition of *conformist bias* in the footnotes for Reading B. What are some examples of conformist bias in human society? Discuss with a partner and note your ideas.

Girls wear pink/purple
Boys wear blue
Clothes style- holes in jean

COMPLETION **A.** Complete the information using the correct form of the words in the box.

aspect	evolve	exchange	human	standard

Parrots and ¹ _human_ learn to vocalize similarly: Both listen and then repeat back what they hear. Now scientists have found another ² _aspect_ of their behavior that is similar. Parrots do not speak a single, ³ _standard_ language; they speak in regional dialects.

A team from New Mexico State University has studied the vocal ⁴ _exchange_ among Amazon parrots living in Costa Rica. All the birds use a specific call to communicate. However, the call varies by region. When one bird hears the local dialect of another, it changes its own call to match the new tune.

Only a few animals have ⁵ _evolved_ to communicate in this way. "Learning how to sound like others is very important to parrots," says researcher Timothy Wright. "When you sound like another, that means you are a member of their group."

^ **A yellow-naped Amazon parrot**

DEFINITIONS **B.** Match the two parts of each definition.

1. If you **create** something,   a. two or more things are joined together.
2. If something is a **combination**,   b. you make something new.
3. If something is **cultural**,   c. it causes a change.
4. If something has an **impact**,   d. it is correct.
5. If information is **accurate**,   e. it relates to the ideas or customs of a particular society.

WORD FORMS **C.** Many nouns, such as **combination**, are formed from verbs by adding the suffix **-tion**.

1. Complete the chart below. Use a dictionary to help.

Verb		Noun
Combine	→	**combination**
create	→	_Creation_
evolve	→	_Evolution_

2. Complete these sentences using the correct form of the words above.

a. To communicate, bees use a(n) _combination_ of body movements and chemical signals.
b. The development of language has played an important role in human _evolution_.
c. Like bees, ants can _create_ chemicals called "pheromones."
d. As a language _envolves_, the meaning of certain words can change.

34 Unit 2B

THE LION'S ROAR

< A lioness roars as her cubs play in Kenya's Maasai Mara National Reserve.

BEFORE YOU WATCH

PREVIEWING

A. Read the information. The words and phrases in bold appear in the video. Match each word with its definition.

The lion is known for its power and strength, as well as its famously fierce roar. In fact, a lion's roar can be as loud as 114 decibels—about as loud as **thunder**. These sounds are made by both lions and lionesses, though lionesses do not roar as often, or as loudly. Male lions—especially the **dominant** lion in the pride (the lion family group)—roar to warn others to leave their **territory**. They also roar to communicate their location to their family; this is called *social roaring*.

1. thunder   •   • a. the loud sound you hear after lightning

2. dominant   •   • b. an area of land belonging to a particular person or group

3. territory   •   • c. more important or powerful than most or all others

QUIZ

B. What do you know about lions? Discuss the questions below with a partner.

1. Which is bigger, a lion or a tiger?

2. What is the name given to a group of lions?

3. Which usually hunts for food—the male or the female lion?

4. In which two continents do lions live today?

GIST   **A.** Watch the video. Check your ideas in Before You Watch B.

COMPLETION   **B.** Watch the video again. Complete the sentences by circling the correct options.

1. Lions are able to roar *as soon as they are born* / *when they are one year old*.

2. There are usually more adult *males* / *females* in a pride of lions.

3. American lions and cave lions became extinct around *1,000* / *10,000* years ago.

4. *African* / *Asiatic* lions are the most endangered lion species today.

CRITICAL THINKING Synthesizing Information

▶ Consider what you have learned about animal communication in this unit. What do you remember about each animal listed below? Discuss with a partner.

| humpback whale | lyrebird | swamp sparrow | parrot | lion |

▶ Imagine you are a scientist who studies animal communication. Which animal would you most like to study? What would you like to find out about it? Why? Note your ideas below. Then discuss with a partner.

_____

_____

_____

VOCABULARY REVIEW

Do you remember the meanings of these words? Check (✓) the ones you know. Look back at the unit and review any words you're not sure of.

Reading A

☐ apparently* ☐ aware* ☐ complex* ☐ curiously ☐ experience

☐ interact* ☐ record ☐ season ☐ single ☐ unknown

Reading B

☐ accurate* ☐ aspect* ☐ combination ☐ create* ☐ cultural*

☐ evolve* ☐ exchange ☐ human ☐ impact* ☐ standard

* Academic Word List

HISTORY DETECTIVES

3

Discuss these questions with a partner.

1. How do scientists learn about the past?

2. What famous historical sites have you visited? What did you see there?

∧ An archeologist examines the inside of a cave in Mallorca, Spain.

3A

BEFORE YOU READ

DEFINITIONS **A.** Look at the photo and read the information below. Match each word in **bold** with its definition.

On November 4, 1922, a British **archeologist** named Howard Carter discovered the **tomb** of King Tutankhamen. Inside, he found a beautiful solid gold **coffin** containing a **mummy**. It was the body of the young Egyptian king who had died over 3,200 years before.

1. archeologist •   • a. a preserved body

2. tomb   •   • b. a room used to bury the dead

3. coffin   •   • c. a box in which a dead body is kept

4. mummy   •   • d. a scientist who studies things and people from the past

SKIMMING **B.** What are some theories about how King Tutankhamen died? Quickly skim the passage. Then compare your ideas with a partner.

WAS KING TUT MURDERED?

A King Tutankhamen was still a teenager when he died around 1322 B.C. He ruled Egypt for ten years, the last king of a powerful family that had ruled the country for centuries. After his death, the body of King Tut (as Tutankhamen is usually known today) was placed in a gold-filled tomb. There, he lay forgotten until the tomb's discovery in 1922. Although we know a lot about his life, the reason for King Tut's death at such a young age has remained a mystery, with **murder** the most extreme possibility. Now, improved X-ray technology[1] and DNA[2] testing are **offering** new clues into the life and death of the boy-king.

Discovered and Damaged

B When British archeologist Howard Carter opened King Tut's tomb, it was full of gold and other amazing items. Carter spent months carefully recording the treasures. When he and his team attempted to remove King Tut's mummy, they found that it had become **attached** to its solid gold coffin. Unfortunately, they **caused** a great deal of damage to the mummy while removing it.

Theories about Tut's Death

C In 1968, archeologists **conducted** an examination of King Tut's mummy using simple X-ray technology. Three important discoveries led to various theories about his death.

- The X-rays showed that bones in Tut's chest[3] were missing. Some guessed the damage was caused by a war **injury** or an accident.
- There was a small hole in the back of the skull, and pieces of bone inside it, causing many to believe that Tut was killed by a blow to the back of the head. Was he murdered by people wanting to **take control of** Egypt?
- A serious fracture was discovered on Tut's left leg. Tut had been hurt a few hours before his death. Could an **infection** from the injury have killed Tut?

---

1 **X-ray technology** is a special way of taking pictures of the inside of something.
2 **DNA** (deoxyribonucleic acid) is the material that carries information on how a living thing will look or function.
3 Your **chest** is the top part of the front of your body.

∧ Tutankhamen's tomb was decorated with colorful paintings of gods and goddesses.

A Closer Look

D In 2005, scientists under the direction of Egyptian archeologist Zahi Hawass used new and more **effective** X-ray technology to study the mummy. They discovered that the damage to Tut's chest was caused by Howard Carter, and the hole in Tut's skull was made when embalmers[4] were preparing the body for burial. While this ruled out one theory—that of murder—it still doesn't tell us exactly how he died.

E Then, in 2008, Hawass and his team **analyzed** Tut's DNA. They found that he suffered from flat feet as well as a bone disease: This would have made it difficult for him to walk. When they analyzed the DNA of the mummies in other tombs nearby, they made some shocking discoveries. They found Tut's father and mother, who had similar DNA, were actually brother and sister. The DNA they passed on to Tut may have left him highly vulnerable to disease, such as malaria.[5] Did an infection that started in his fractured leg—added to the bone disease—cause his death? No one knows for sure. But Hawass and his team hope they will someday have an answer to this age-old mystery.

4 **Embalmers** are people who prepare a body for burial.
5 **Malaria** is a serious disease that is carried by mosquitoes.

Through CT scans of King Tut's mummy, scientists are learning more and more about how the boy-king lived, and how he might have died.

INSIDE KING TUT'S TOMB

The tomb of Tutankhamen was found hidden in the Valley of the Kings. Although some of its outer rooms were robbed in ancient times, the tomb itself was not opened. Inside were walls decorated with colorful paintings and nine layers of wood, stone, and gold, protecting the body of the king.

To reach King Tut's mummy, Carter and his team had to remove four huge boxes, or shrines. Each shrine was made from heavy wood and covered with golden pictures of Egyptian gods.

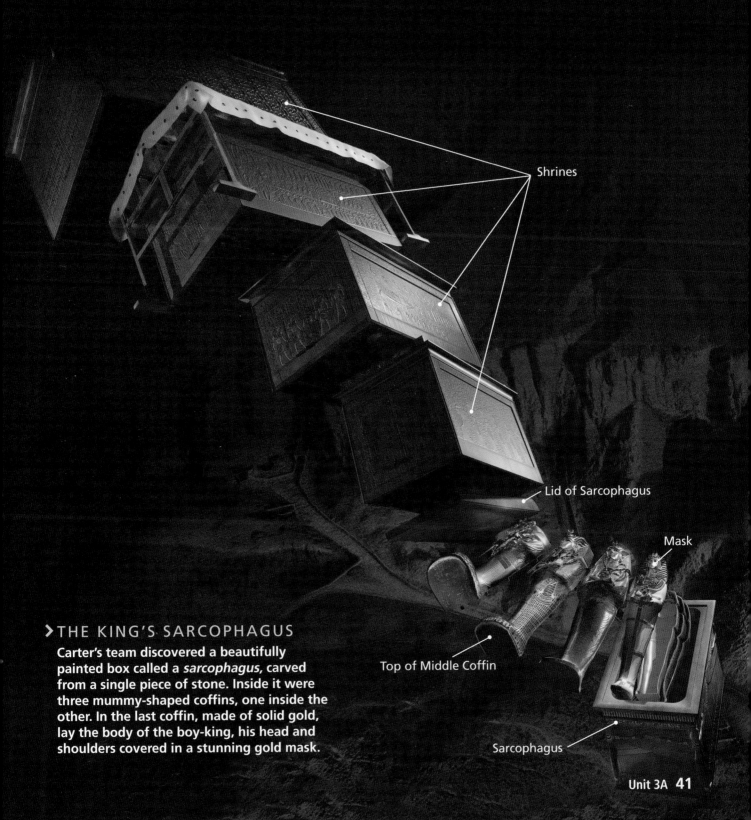

Shrines

Lid of Sarcophagus

Mask

Top of Middle Coffin

Sarcophagus

❯ THE KING'S SARCOPHAGUS

Carter's team discovered a beautifully painted box called a *sarcophagus,* carved from a single piece of stone. Inside it were three mummy-shaped coffins, one inside the other. In the last coffin, made of solid gold, lay the body of the boy-king, his head and shoulders covered in a stunning gold mask.

A. Choose the best answer for each question.

GIST

1. How does the passage answer the question, "Was King Tut murdered?"

   a. He was probably murdered.
   b. He almost certainly died in an accident.
   c. How he died is still not known.

DETAIL

2. King Tut's skull was damaged ___.

   a. by the new X-ray technology
   b. when it was removed from the coffin
   c. when the mummy was prepared for burial

VOCABULARY

3. In paragraph D, the phrase *ruled out* is closest in meaning to ___.

   a. suggested
   b. confirmed
   c. rejected

More than 130 canes and walking sticks were found inside King Tut's tomb. Many showed signs of use. This suggests that Tut was unable to walk properly.

DETAIL

4. Which of the following did Carter NOT find in Tut's tomb?

   a. colorful paintings
   b. King Tut's parents
   c. a golden mask

DETAIL

5. What did scientists discover by analyzing King Tut's DNA?

   a. He suffered from a bone disease.
   b. He had an infection in his leg.
   c. He had a brother and a sister.

REFERENCE

Review this reading skill in Unit 2A

B. Find these pronouns in the passage. What does each one refer to? Note your answers.

1. *it* (paragraph B, line 2) — King Tut's tomb
2. *it* (paragraph B, line 6) — The mummy
3. *it* (paragraph C, line 8) — The back of the skull
4. *he* (paragraph D, line 6) — King tut
5. *they* (paragraph E, line 6) — Tut's Parents
6. *they* (paragraph E, line 9) — Hawas and his team

Creating a Timeline of Events

When you read a text that describes a series of events, it can be useful to place the events on a timeline. This provides you with a clear picture of the important events in the order they happened. A timeline can be used for events that occurred on specific dates, as well as for events that cover a period of time.

SCANNING **A.** Find and underline these events in Reading A.

a. King Tut's DNA is analyzed.
b. King Tut begins his rule of Egypt.
c. King Tut is placed in a gold-filled tomb.
d. Howard Carter discovers King Tut's tomb.
e. Outer rooms of King Tut's tomb are robbed.
f. King Tut's family, a series of powerful kings, ruled Egypt.
g. More effective X-ray technology is applied to the mummies.
h. Images of King Tut's mummy are taken with simple X-ray technology.

⌃ **The golden mask of Tutankhamen**

UNDERSTANDING SEQUENCE **B.** Label the timeline with the events above.

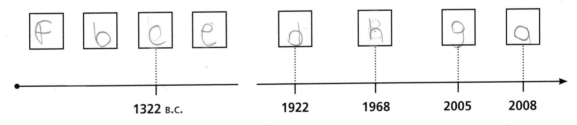

| f | b | c | e | | d | h | g | a |

1322 B.C.   1922   1968   2005   2008

CRITICAL THINKING Justifying Opinions   Do you think it is important that we find out how King Tut died? Why or why not? Note your ideas below. Then discuss with a partner.

_____

_____

_____

_____

COMPLETION   **A.** Complete the information using the words in the box. Two words are extra.

analyze	attached	cause	conduct
effective	infection	murder	offer

A group of 700-year-old mummies unearthed in Handong, South Korea, has provided researchers with some interesting findings. The mummies may ¹ _____offer_____ hope for treating a deadly modern-day illness, and they also tell of an ancient love story.

One of the bodies found showed signs of ² _____Infections_____ with the hepatitis B virus. Scientists hope that after they ³ _____analyze_____ the body, they will better understand the disease, and find more ⁴ _____effective_____ ways to treat it.

Another mummy was a young man who may have been involved in a plan to ⁵ _____murder_____ the emperor. He was found buried with poems written by his wife. The 500-year-old poems show how strongly ⁶ _____attached_____ she was to her husband, even beyond his death.

> **A mummy found in South Korea in 2007 had a poem buried with him that reads:**
> *I cannot live without you anymore. I wish I could be with you. Please let me go with you. My love to you, it is unforgettable in this world, and my sorrow, it is without end.*

DEFINITIONS   **B.** Complete the sentences. Circle the correct words.

1. She suffered a(n) (**injury**) / **murder** to her ankle as she stepped out of the car.

2. The archeologists (**conducted**) / **caused** a series of tests on the mummy.

3. Thousands of years ago, the Roman Empire (**took control of**) / **offered** many parts of Europe.

4. The (**cause**) / **murder** of the accident remains under investigation.

WORD FORMS   **C.** Some words, like **cause**, can act as both a noun and a verb.

What exactly was the **cause** *of death? Did the infection* **cause** *this death?*

Write two sentences for each word, first as a noun and then as a verb.

1. offer

_____Stores offer TVs on Black Friday_____

_____

2. murder

_____The movie was about a murder ____

_____

BEFORE YOU READ

DISCUSSION **A.** A mummy, known as the "Iceman," was found high in the Alps in Italy in 1991. Look at the picture and read the caption. Then discuss the questions with a partner.

    1. What kind of man do you think the "Iceman" was?

    2. Where and when did he die? What do you think happened to him?

SCANNING **B.** Scan the reading passage to see if your predictions in activity A were correct.

Review this reading skill in Unit 2B

DESCRIPTION OF BODY:
Male, mid-forties
Died 5,300 years ago
Possessions: three layers of clothes, bearskin shoes, stone knife, copper ax, wooden arrows
Condition: deep cuts on hand and one on back, dark object visible under skin of left shoulder

⌄ **A model of the "Iceman," who was found frozen in the Alps**

WHO KILLED THE ICEMAN?

A In 1991, high in the mountains of Europe, hikers made a shocking discovery: a dead man partly **frozen** in the ice. The police investigation soon became a scientific one. Carbon dating[1] **indicated** that the man died over 5,300 years ago. Today, he is known as the Iceman and nicknamed "Ötzi" for the Ötztal Alps where he was found. Kept in perfect condition by the ice, he is the oldest complete human body found on Earth.

Who Was the Iceman?

B Scientists believe Ötzi was an important person in his village. Examinations of his teeth and skull tell us he was in his mid-forties when he died. The things he carried also tell us about who he was. His knife was made of stone, but he carried a copper[2] ax. This was a valuable tool in Ötzi's time and suggests that he may have been a local **leader**. A fire-starting kit was discovered with him, so we know he could make fire. And the food he ate and carried **enabled** scientists to know exactly where in Italy he lived—a village down in the valley.

Clues to an Ancient Murder

C But why did Ötzi die in such a high and icy place? Some said he was a lost farmer or shepherd.[3] Others thought he was killed in a religious ceremony. No one knows for sure.

D Over the years, tiny scientific discoveries have led to great changes in our understanding of Ötzi's story. "[Once], the story was that he **fled** up there and walked around in the snow and probably died of exposure,"[4] said scientist Klaus Oeggl. "Now it's all changed. … It's more like a … crime scene."

---

1 **Carbon dating** is a scientific method of finding out how old an object is.

2 **Copper** is a soft, reddish brown metal.

3 A **shepherd** is a person who takes care of sheep.

4 **Exposure** is the harmful effect on your body from very cold weather.

A Bloody Discovery

E In fact, the newest scientific information indicates Ötzi was **cruelly** murdered. In June 2001, an X-ray of the body showed a small dark shape **beneath** Ötzi's left shoulder. It was the stone head of an arrow that had hit him from behind. CT scans showed that this caused an injury that killed him very quickly.

F Then, in 2003, an Australian scientist discovered the blood of four other people on Ötzi's clothes. Was Ötzi killed in a fight? It isn't **likely**, as Ötzi's other injuries, on his hand and head, had already started to close. This means there probably was a fight, but it happened much earlier.

G Perhaps Ötzi was being **chased** when he died? In 2010, scientists took the mummy out of the cold and examined him again. They discovered that just before his death, he had a big meal of bread and goat meat. In 2018, further analysis of his stomach showed Ötzi had also eaten deer meat. Would someone being chased stop to eat a large meal? The scientists don't think so. More likely, he was **attacked** while resting. He may have thought he had escaped and was safe. Today, the research continues, proving some of these ideas as false while opening the door to others. Ötzi, it seems, has more to tell us about his life and the time in which he lived.

In his last moments, the Iceman, Ötzi, lay in the cold, alone. There his body stayed for thousands of years.

A. Choose the best answer for each question.

GIST

1. What was the most likely cause of Ötzi's death?
- a. He was killed in a religious ceremony.
- b. He was chased and killed during a fight.
- c. He was attacked from behind while resting.

DETAIL

2. Which is the best description of Ötzi?
- a. an important man from a village in Italy
- b. a poor farmer who lived in the mountains
- c. a young man who made weapons

DETAIL

3. What caused the death of the Iceman?
- a. a knife
- b. an arrow
- c. the cold

DETAIL

4. Why is it believed that a fight took place long before Ötzi's death?
- a. No weapons were found on his body.
- b. He was bleeding from his shoulder.
- c. Injuries on his hand and head had begun to close.

VOCABULARY

5. In paragraph G, what does *opening the door to* mean?
- a. allowing for the possibility of
- b. disproving the idea of
- c. providing a reason for

⌃ **A life-size model of the Iceman at the South Tyrol Museum of Archeology in Bolzano, Italy**

CREATING A TIMELINE

Review this reading skill in Unit 3A

B. Add the events (a–e) to complete the timeline.
- a. An X-ray showed a dark shape beneath Ötzi's left shoulder.
- b. A scientist discovered the blood of other people on Ötzi's clothes.
- c. Scientists found that Ötzi had eaten deer before he died.
- d. Scientists learned that Ötzi had eaten bread and goat before he died.
- e. The police investigation of Ötzi became a scientific investigation.

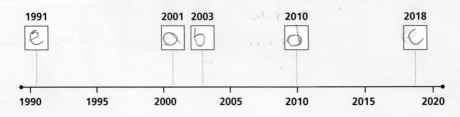

1991 — e
2001 — a
2003 — b
2010 — d
2018 — c

1990 1995 2000 2005 2010 2015 2020

Distinguishing Facts from Speculation

Scientific and historical texts often contain a mix of both facts and speculation.

Facts are ideas that are known to be true, or that can be proven. For example, the idea that Ötzi died over 5,300 years ago (paragraph A) is considered a fact because it can be proven by carbon dating.

Speculation refers to ideas that have not been proven to be true or false. Words that indicate speculation include *think, believe, may, might, could, possibly, probably, perhaps,* and *(un)likely.*

SCANNING **A.** Look back at Reading B. Find this information about Ötzi and underline it in the text.

F   E   **1.** He was found in the mountains.

S   F   **2.** He died over 5,300 years ago.

    S   **3.** He was an important person in his village.

    F   **4.** Blood from four people was found on his clothes.

    F   **5.** He had injuries on his hand and head.

    S   **6.** A bloody fight took place before his murder.

    S   **7.** He was being chased following a fight.

    E   **8.** He ate meat and bread before he died.

    S   **9.** He was resting when he was attacked.

    S   **10.** He thought he was safe when he was attacked.

The Iceman is hit in the shoulder by a stone arrow. Scientists believe this is what killed him.

DISTINGUISHING FACTS FROM SPECULATION **B.** Which of the statements above are facts (**F**), and which are speculation (**S**)? Write **F** or **S** next to each statement. Then circle the words and phrases in the reading that indicate speculation.

CRITICAL THINKING Evaluating Evidence

▶ For each piece of speculation mentioned above, what supporting evidence does the author give? Look back at Reading B and circle any supporting evidence.

▶ Discuss with a partner. How well supported is each claim? Are there any other possible explanations?

VOCABULARY PRACTICE

DEFINITIONS **A.** Read the information below. Then complete the definitions using the correct form of the words in **red**.

What **enabled** the Iceman's body to survive for over 5,000 years? Scientists thought Ötzi's body may have dried out, like mummies in Egypt. However, Egyptian mummies still have hair, and Ötzi's did not. This difference **indicates** that the body had been preserved by a different process. Bodies that stay in water for a long time lose their hair. So it is **likely** that Ötzi's body was underwater before it was **frozen** in the ice.

1. If something is ___likely___ to happen, it will probably happen.
2. To ___enabled___ something means to suggest or show it to be true.
3. If something is ___frozen___, it has become very hard because of the cold.
4. If you ___indicates___ something to happen, you help make it possible.

COMPLETION **B.** Complete the information with the correct form of the words in the box.

attack	beneath	chase	cruel	flee	leader

1. Ötzi's killers probably ___attacked___ him while he was resting.
2. In Ötzi's time, a ___leader___ carried better equipment than ordinary men.
3. Ötzi's mummy was buried ___beneath___ the ice and snow for thousands of years.
4. It is unlikely that someone ___chase___ the Iceman up the mountain. Evidence suggests Ötzi had stopped to eat a meal.
5. It is possible that Ötzi ___fleed___ to the mountain because of something that happened earlier.
6. Ötzi's attackers were ___cruel___ to leave him to die in the cold.

COLLOCATIONS **C.** The nouns in the box are frequently used with the adjective **cruel**. Complete the sentences using the correct words.

act	comment	death	trick

1. The murder of Ötzi was a really cruel ___act___.
2. The Iceman suffered a cruel ___death___ out in the cold.
3. The children played a cruel ___trick___ on their parents.
4. In the morning, he was sorry for the cruel ___comment___ he'd posted online.

WALKING WITH GIANTS

⌄ Moai statues on the
Pacific island of Rapa Nui

BEFORE YOU WATCH

PREVIEWING **A.** Read the information. The words in **bold** appear in the video. Match each word with its definition.

Rapa Nui (also known as Easter Island) is home to over 900 *moai* statues. Around 1,000 years ago, these huge figures were **carved** from stone that came from many kilometers away. No one knows for sure how the ancient Rapa Nui moved them. Over the years, many different theories have been suggested. Some believe that **aliens** moved them; the traditional Rapa Nui story is that the statues came alive and walked across the island. In recent years, however, more scientific **approaches** have been taken in an attempt to solve the mystery.

1. carve — a. a method or way of doing something

2. aliens — b. creatures or people not from Earth

3. approach — c. to make something by cutting a material like wood or stone

DISCUSSION **B.** What are some possible ways the ancient Rapa Nui could have moved the moai statues? Discuss your ideas with a partner.

GIST **A.** Watch the video. How were the moai moved? Match each theory with the correct description.

1. 1955 theory •   • a. Moai were placed on a sled on top of rolling logs.
2. 1970 theory •   • b. Moai were standing and moved with a twisting motion.
3. 1986 theory •   • c. Moai were carried using a V-shaped frame.
4. 1987 theory •   • d. Moai were dragged on top of tree trunks.
5. 2011 theory •   • e. Moai were moved by three groups of people with ropes.

DETAIL **B.** Watch the video again. Choose the best answer for each question.

1. According to some, why is the 1970 theory unlikely to be correct?

   a. because a full-size model was never built and tested

   b. because traditional stories say that the moai "walked"

2. What gave Terry Hunt and Carl Lipo the idea for their 2011 theory?

   a. They discovered the bottoms of the statues were not flat.

   b. They realized all the moai statues were located near ancient roads.

3. In Hunt and Lipo's 2011 theory, how were the three groups of people arranged?

   a. One group was in front of the statue, and the other two were behind it.

   b. One group was behind the statue, and the other two were at each side.

CRITICAL THINKING Evaluating Evidence   What evidence mentioned in the video supports the 2011 theory? How well supported is it? Note your ideas, then discuss with a partner.

_____

VOCABULARY REVIEW

Do you remember the meanings of these words? Check (✓) the ones you know. Look back at the unit and review any words you're not sure of.

Reading A

☐ analyze*   ☐ attached*   ☐ cause   ☐ conduct*   ☐ effective

☐ infection   ☐ injury*   ☐ murder   ☐ offer   ☐ take control of

Reading B

☐ attack   ☐ beneath   ☐ chase   ☐ cruelly   ☐ enable*

☐ flee   ☐ frozen   ☐ indicate* ☐ leader   ☐ likely

* Academic Word List

TRADITIONS AND RITUALS

4

Folk dancers in traditional costume at a local festival in Trujillo, Peru

WARM UP

Discuss these questions with a partner.

1. What are some important traditions in your culture?

2. What is your favorite tradition? Why?

53

4A

DISCUSSION
A. Read the first paragraph of the passage and discuss these questions with a partner.

   1. Can you name any other places on the UNESCO World Heritage sites list?

   2. Why do you think many of these places and areas need protection?

SKIMMING

Review this
reading skill
in Unit 1A

B. Skim the other paragraphs. What do you think the reading is mainly about? Circle a, b, or c. Then read the passage to check your answer.

   a. the most famous UNESCO World Heritage sites

   b. a UNESCO list for important cultural traditions

   c. how UNESCO has changed since it first began

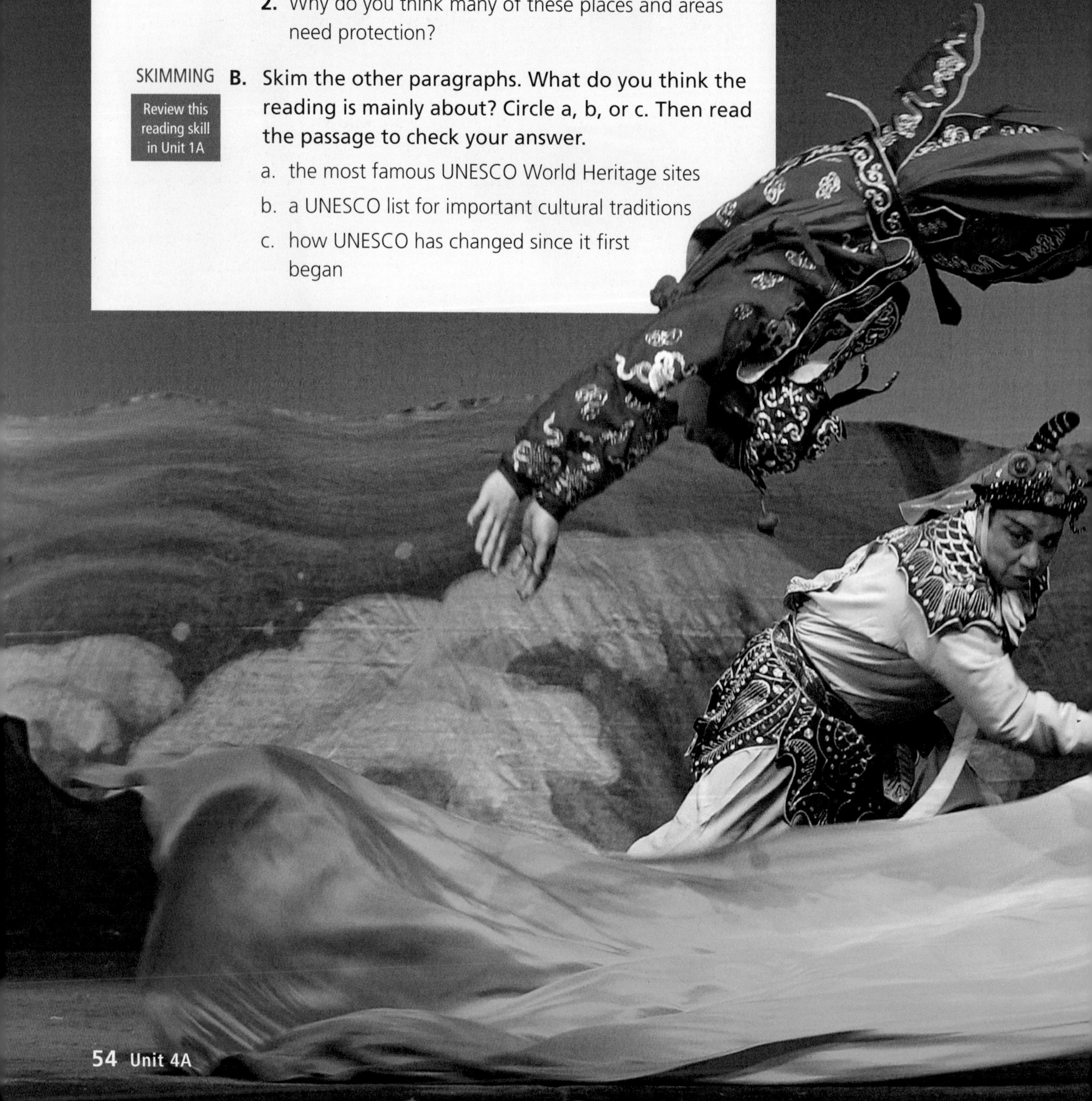

A performance of *The Legend of the White Snake* by the China National Peking Opera Company

LIVING
TREASURES

A The Tower of Pisa. Machu Picchu. The Taj Mahal. You probably know them as famous UNESCO[1] World Heritage **sites**—structures and monuments of great cultural value. But what about the Mediterranean diet? The Beijing opera? Or the art of pizza-making in Naples? What do these have in common?

B Traditions like these are known as "intangible cultural heritage." In contrast to UNESCO World Heritage sites, intangible heritage does not include buildings like palaces and temples. Instead, it includes traditional art forms, such as music, dance, and **craft**-making—living traditions that are an important part of a place's culture.

C UNESCO began to identify cultural traditions in 2008. Among the first on their list were the Puppet Theater of Sicily and Mexico's Day of the Dead festival. By 2017, UNESCO had **approved** more than 300 **diverse** practices. These include cultural events like the Chinese Dragon Boat Festival; performing arts including Spanish flamenco; martial arts such as Brazilian capoeira and Korean Taekkyeon; and handicrafts like Japanese washi paper-making.

D In 2010, UNESCO also began to include important regional cuisines, starting with French and Mexican food. Several other types of food and drink have since been added, such as Korean kimchi and Croatian gingerbread. Arabic coffee was included in 2015. The sharing of coffee has been an important aspect of Arab hospitality for centuries, according to UNESCO, and is "a **symbol** of generosity."

---

1 The **United Nations Educational, Scientific, and Cultural Organization** helps nations work together in the fields of education, culture, and science.

Protecting Cultural Roots

E Cultural rituals are an important part of the UNESCO list. An example is the Tlemcen **wedding** ritual in Algeria. The ritual begins in the bride's parents' home, where friends and female relatives help the bride prepare for the **ceremony**. The bride is first dressed in a golden silk dress. Symbolic henna[2] designs are applied to her hands. Before leaving the house for the ceremony, her face is **wrapped** in a golden silk veil.[3] Later, during the wedding feast, the bride removes her veil, ready to be married. The tradition has passed from one generation to the next, and marks the community's cultural **identity**.

F Some of the cultural items on the list are dying out and in need of protection. An example is Al Sadu—traditional weaving in the United Arab Emirates. The tradition was once widely practiced by communities of desert Bedouin women. However, many Bedouin have now moved to cities, and so the practice has begun to disappear. Today, Al Sadu is mostly practiced by older women whose numbers are declining.

G The main goal of UNESCO is to **promote** peace through respect for the world's varied cultures and common humanity. It hopes that by bringing attention to cultural traditions such as Al Sadu, they will be more likely to survive. Cultural traditions are important to fight for, says Cécile Duvelle of UNESCO. "The more globalized the world becomes," she says, "the more important it is not to lose these traditional roots."

> Algerian women decorate a bride's hands with henna during a Tlemcen wedding.

2 **Henna** is a type of dye often used for coloring hair and skin.
3 A **veil** is a thin piece of material that covers the face.

READING COMPREHENSION

A. Choose the best answer for each question.

PURPOSE

1. What is the purpose of paragraph B?
   a. to describe the most famous World Heritage sites
   b. to provide details about the history of UNESCO
   c. to give a definition of "intangible cultural heritage"

An Algerian bride dances with her relatives during her wedding party.

DETAIL

2. Which of the following was one of the first items added to the intangible cultural heritage list?
   a. Arabic coffee
   b. Korean kimchi
   c. Sicilian Puppet Theater

INFERENCE

3. Which of the following could NOT be added to the intangible cultural heritage list?
   a. flute music from Peru
   b. a historic bridge in Paris
   c. an Irish poetry festival

DETAIL

4. Which of the following is true about a Tlemcen wedding?
   a. The main ceremony takes place in the bride's parents' home.
   b. Female family members help the bride prepare for the event.
   c. The bride takes off her veil before leaving the house.

PURPOSE

5. Why does the author mention Al Sadu?
   a. to show that traditional weaving is still popular in Bedouin culture
   b. to give an example of an intangible item that could soon disappear
   c. to show how the UNESCO list is already achieving success

SCANNING

Review this reading skill in Unit 2B

B. Scan the reading for each of the intangible cultural items listed below (1–7). Match each one with the correct category (a–d).

a. Regional food and drink   b. Performing arts   c. Handicrafts   d. Cultural events

1. Al Sadu ____ C
2. Arabic coffee ____ a
3. Dragon Boat Festival ____ d
4. Flamenco ____ b
5. Mediterranean diet ____ a
6. Tlemcen wedding ritual ____ d
7. Washi ____ C

Dealing with Unfamiliar Vocabulary (1)—Using Context

If a word or phrase in a text is unfamiliar, you may be able to understand its meaning from the context. Look at the words around it and try to guess the meaning. Are there any examples that help you understand what it means? In some cases, the meaning may be explained in the text. Definitions are often set off by commas, a dash (—), or dashes:

> An example is Al Sadu—traditional weaving in the United Arab Emirates.

The writer may also explain the meaning using words or phrases like *means, is called,* or *known as.* At other times, a word may be defined in a glossary or a footnote.

SCANNING **A.** These words and phrases appear in the reading passage. Find and circle them.

> **cuisine   martial art   ritual   roots   veil**

MATCHING **B.** Use the context to help you identify the meaning of each word or phrase. Then match each word with its definition (a–e).

1. cuisine   a. a fixed set of actions, often relating to religion

2. martial art   b. the place or culture that a person comes from

3. ritual   c. a piece of thin material worn over the face

4. roots   d. a method of fighting or self-defense

5. veil   e. the style of cooking common in a certain place

CRITICAL THINKING Applying Ideas

▶ Work with a partner. List some examples of intangible cultural heritage from your country. Note at least one idea for each category.

Cuisine	Performing Arts	Crafts	Cultural Events
Corundas	Bolle de los viejitos	figurines	Doy of the dead

▶ Imagine you can select only one item from your list to be included on UNESCO's list. Which would you choose? Note your ideas and reasons, and share with a partner.

The unesco will need include the crafts from mexico like the ollas.

COMPLETION **A.** Complete the information using the correct form of the words in the box.
One word is extra.

> approve   ceremony   site   symbol   wedding   wrap

The Wodaabe are nomadic African people who migrate
from place to place throughout the year. At the end
of September, the Wodaabe come together for an
important cultural ¹ _Ceremony_ called the
geerewol. The ritual includes a unique beauty contest.
Young Wodaabe men paint their faces with makeup, and
² _warp_ their heads in colorful headwear.
Some put on beads and shells as ³ _symbol_
of their wealth. They then perform a dance for young
Wodaabe women. If a woman ⁴ _approve_ of a
male dancer, she may agree to marry him and a
⁵ _wedding_ is prepared.

**A Wodaabe man dressed
in makeup for the
geerewol festival**

COMPLETION **B.** Complete the sentences using the words in the box. One word is extra.

> crafts   diverse   identity   promote   site   wrap

1. The Great Wall of China is a very famous World Heritage _site_ .
2. UNESCO's intangible heritage list includes a(n) _diverse_ range of
   traditional _crafts_ and other art forms.
3. The tradition of flamenco is an important part of Spain's cultural _identity_ .
4. UNESCO's aim is to _promote_ education, science, and culture worldwide.

WORD PARTS **C.** The prefix *pro-* can mean "forward" or "toward the front," as in the verb
promote. Complete the definitions by circling the correct options.

1. If you **proceed with** something, you *make a start on it / decide to change it.*
2. If you **get a promotion**, you *rise to a higher level / move to a different place.*
3. If you **make progress** on something, you *decide to do it / have success with it.*

BEFORE YOU READ

DEFINITIONS **A.** Look at the photo and read the caption. Complete the sentences using the correct form of the words in **bold**.

1. A(n) _monk_ is a member of a male religious community.
2. _acrobatics_ are skillful, athletic movements such as jumping, rolling, etc.
3. A(n) _temple_ is a building for the practice of a religion.
4. A(n) _master_ of something knows how to do it extremely well.

IDENTIFYING PURPOSE **B.** Skim the first three paragraphs of the reading passage. Match each paragraph with its purpose.

Review this reading skill in Unit 1B

1. Paragraph A •   • a. to describe modern kung fu schools in Dengfeng
2. Paragraph B •   • b. to give a brief history of kung fu
3. Paragraph C •   • c. to introduce the owner of a small kung fu school

THE CHANGING FACE OF KUNG FU

A In the fifth century—according to legend—an Indian master taught some monks at the Shaolin Temple a **series** of exercises, or forms, **inspired** by the movements of animals. These forms became the **basis** for the style of fighting known as kung fu. Over 16 centuries, the monks have used kung fu for self-defense and in war. With it, they have won many battles against their enemies.

B In Dengfeng today, ten kilometers from the Shaolin Temple, there are over 60 martial arts schools with more than 50,000 students. They come to the schools for a variety of reasons. Some hope to become movie stars. Others come to learn skills that will **ensure** good jobs in the military or police force. A few are sent by their parents to learn self-control and hard work.

C Master Hu Zhengsheng teaches at a small school in Dengfeng. Recently, he was offered an important role in a kung fu movie. It would have been good **publicity** for his school, but he did not **accept**. He doesn't agree with how kung fu is often shown in movies. He feels they show too much **violence**.

D Unlike many large schools, which teach acrobatics and kickboxing, Hu teaches his students traditional kung fu forms. He teaches them the way his master—a Shaolin legend—taught him. But attracting new students to this style of kung fu has become a problem. Hu is afraid his art will soon die out. He has to **remind** his students that kung fu was designed for fighting, not to entertain.

E "There are no high kicks or acrobatics here," he says. "It is hard to **convince** boys to spend many years learning something that won't make them wealthy or famous."

F Hu's students have little. They sleep in unheated rooms and train outside no matter what the temperature. They hit trees with their bare hands and take turns sitting on each other's shoulders to build leg strength. Why such hardship? To master kung fu, they must learn **respect**, and how to "eat bitterness," a Mandarin expression meaning "to endure suffering." The life of a Shaolin master, Hu teaches, is not easy or attractive.

G Master Hu is in a difficult position. For old traditions to survive, the young must learn. Gradually, he has begun offering a few courses in kickboxing and the acrobatic kung fu forms, hoping to attract new students. Then, maybe, he'll be able to convince them to learn Shaolin kung fu the traditional way.

The Shaolin **Temple** has stood in the mountains of China's Henan Province for over 1,500 years. The **monks** who live there are **masters** of a martial art called *kung fu*. In movies, kung fu usually involves lots of **acrobatics**, which is not taught in more traditional styles of kung fu.

A. Choose the best answer for each question.

GIST

1. What is the reading mainly about?

    a. a kung fu student learning kickboxing

    (b.) a kung fu master preserving old traditions

    c. a famous actor who studied kung fu

DETAIL

2. Which is NOT given as a reason why people study kung fu?

    (a.) to think more clearly

    b. to help get jobs

    c. to become movie stars

REFERENCE

3. In paragraph E, what does *here* refer to?

    a. in kung fu movies

    b. in the city of Dengfeng

    (c.) in Master Hu's school

PARAPHRASING

4. Which of the following is closest in meaning to *no matter what the temperature* (paragraph F)?

    (a.) even if it's very hot or cold

    b. only when the temperature is hot

    c. because it's warmer than in their rooms

▽ **A Shaolin monk displays his soccer skills.**

VOCABULARY

5. In paragraph F, what does *endure suffering* mean?

    (a.) stop the suffering

    b. make someone suffer

    c. survive the suffering

EVALUATING STATEMENTS

B. Are the following statements true or false according to the reading passage, or is the information not given? Circle **T** (true), **F** (false), or **NG** (not given).

1. Kung fu is believed to be over 2,000 years old.   T   F   (NG)

2. The easiest animal form to learn is the tiger.   T   (F)   (NG)

3. China's most famous actor studied in Dengfeng.   (T)   F   NG

4. Master Hu learned kung fu by watching movies.   T   (F)   NG

5. Master Hu's students have to cook their own meals.   T   (F)   (NG)

6. Hu has started to give classes in kickboxing.   (T)   F   NG

Differentiating Between Main Ideas and Supporting Details

A paragraph usually has one main idea—the most important piece of information. To find the main idea, ask yourself, "What is this paragraph mainly about?" or "What point is the author trying to make?"

A paragraph is developed around this main idea. Supporting sentences may give reasons and other details, provide examples or definitions, and make comparisons or contrasts.

IDENTIFYING
MAIN IDEAS
AND DETAILS

A. Look back at the reading passage. In each pair of sentences below, identify the main idea (**M**) of the paragraph and the supporting sentence (**S**).

Paragraph A
   a. __S__ With it, they have won many battles against their enemies.
   b. __M__ These forms became the basis for the style of fighting known as kung fu.

Paragraph B
   a. __M__ Students come to the schools for a variety of reasons.
   b. __S__ Some hope to become movie stars.

Paragraph C
   a. __S__ He feels they (movies) show too much violence.
   b. __M__ He doesn't agree with how kung fu is often shown in movies.

Paragraph D
   a. __S__ He has to remind his students that kung fu was designed for fighting, not to entertain.
   b. __M__ Unlike many large schools, which teach acrobatics and kickboxing, Hu teaches his students traditional kung fu forms.

Paragraph F
   a. __S__ They sleep in unheated rooms and train outside no matter what the temperature.
   b. __M__ The life of a Shaolin master, Hu teaches, is not easy or attractive.

CRITICAL THINKING Relating Information

▶ List some traditional practices in your country that are changing.

_____

_____

▶ Choose one of the practices. How is it changing? Are the changes for the better? Discuss your ideas with a partner.

COMPLETION   **A.** Complete the information using the words in the box.

> basis   convinced   ensured   inspired   series

Many kung fu forms were ¹ _Inspired_ by the movements of animals, like the snake, crane, or tiger. The monks studied how these creatures rested, hunted, and fought. Then, using the animals' behavior as a(n) ² _basis_, the monks created a(n) ³ _Series_ of animal-like fighting styles. According to legend, as some monks studied an animal, they became ⁴ _Convinced_ that they were like that animal. For that reason, they were not allowed to train in any one animal style for too long. Training in several styles also ⁵ _ensured_ that the monks developed a variety of kung fu skills.

Another animal style of kung fu is based on the movements of the praying mantis.

DEFINITIONS   **B.** Complete the definitions. Circle the correct options.

1. You **remind** someone about something so they (don't forget) / can learn about it.

2. One way to **accept** someone's offer is to say, ("Yes, please.") / "No, thanks."

3. **Violence** is behavior that is meant to calm and relax / (hurt or kill.)

4. Someone who is looking for **publicity** wants (to attract) / avoid the public's attention.

5. If you have **respect** for someone, you have a low / (high) opinion of them.

WORD PARTS   **C.** As in **ensure**, the prefix **en-** means "make or cause." It can be added to some adjectives to make verbs. Complete the sentences using the words in the box.

> able   large   rich

1. Traveling abroad can **en** _rich_ your understanding of other cultures.
2. Learning a martial art will **en** _able_ you to defend yourself better.
3. The school needed to **en** _large_ its cafeteria to cope with an increase in student numbers.

> Participants race dragon boats as part of a festival in Shenzhen, China.

DRAGON BOAT
FESTIVAL

BEFORE YOU WATCH

PREVIEWING **A.** Read the information. The words in **bold** appear in the video. Complete the definitions by circling the correct words.

No one really knows how the Chinese Dragon Boat Festival began. However, many people believe it was following the death of a Chinese poet named Qu Yuan. When Qu Yuan fell into a river and disappeared, local people **paddled** down the river in boats searching for his body. The festival is now celebrated every year in countries around the world. While **customs** vary, many festivals feature **intense** dragon boat races. Members of winning teams are thought to receive good luck in the following year.

1. You need to **paddle** in order to *get in / move* a dragon boat.

2. A **custom** is an activity people *rarely / regularly* do.

3. If a feeling is **intense**, it is *not very / very* strong.

GIST **A.** Watch the video. Check (✓) the topics that are mentioned.

✓ a. when the Dragon Boat Festival is held   ☐ d. where the first festival was held

✓ b. the size of dragon boats   ✓ e. what food is eaten at the festival

☐ c. how dragon boats are made   ☐ f. why the boats are dragon-shaped

TRUE OR FALSE **B.** Watch the video again. Circle **T** (true), **F** (false), or **NG** (not given).

1. The longest dragon boats are around sixty meters.	T **(F)** NG
2. The drummer helps control the speed of the boats.	**(T)** F NG
3. The winners of the Xi'an tournament receive a special prize.	T F NG
4. At many festivals, people can learn how to make zongzi.	T F NG
5. The Dragon Boat Festival is a public holiday in China.	T F NG

CRITICAL THINKING Applying Ideas   Work with a partner. Think of an important person or event in your country's history. Design a festival to commemorate this person or event. Note your ideas and include reasons for your choice.

Festival name: _____

Purpose: To commemorate _____

When: _____

Activities: _____

_____

Reason: _____

VOCABULARY REVIEW

Do you remember the meanings of these words? Check (✓) the ones you know. Look back at the unit and review any words you're not sure of.

Reading A

☐ approve   ☐ ceremony   ☐ craft   ☐ diverse*   ☐ identity*

☐ promote*   ☐ site*   ☐ symbol*   ☐ wedding   ☐ wrap

Reading B

☐ accept   ☐ basis   ☐ convince*   ☐ ensure*   ☐ inspire

☐ publicity   ☐ remind   ☐ respect   ☐ series*   ☐ violence

* Academic Word List

FINDING WONDERS

5

Scientists hunt for discoveries in the rocks of Svalbard, Norway.

WARM UP

Discuss these questions with a partner.

1. Why do you think scientists are interested in finding objects underground? What kinds of objects might be useful?

2. Think about the area you live in. What do you think it was like before humans lived there?

67

BEFORE YOU READ

DEFINITIONS **A.** Read the paragraph below. Match each word in **bold** with its definition.

The "Jurassic Coast" in south England has been described as a walk through time. Over millions of years, it has been a desert, a warm sea, and a thick forest. The changes can be seen in rock layers in cliffs along the **beach**. The coastline here is especially famous for its fossils of **extinct** animals—remains of **creatures** that died out long ago. Many are now kept in **museums**. Some have just a few bones, while others show a complete **skeleton**.

1. _____ (adj) no longer living; died out
2. _____ (n) animals (not human beings)
3. _____ (n) a sandy area along the edge of the sea
4. _____ (n) the set of bones inside an animal's body
5. _____ (n) buildings with many cultural or scientific objects

SKIMMING / PREDICTING **B.** Read the first sentence of each paragraph of Reading A. Why do you think Mary Anning is remembered today? Discuss with a partner and check your ideas as you read.

⌃ The cliffs and beach of Lulworth Cove form part of England's Jurassic Coast.

THE SECRETS IN THE SAND

A In 1823, a young woman **noticed** a strange fossil on a beach near Lyme Regis, England. She dug out the bones and had them carried to her home. She carefully **arranged** the skeleton on a table. Then she saw something **extraordinary**. The creature's neck was a meter long—more than half the length of its body. It was unlike any animal living on Earth.

B Even at a young age, Mary Anning had a **talent** for spotting "curies"—unusual or curious, fossils. Her father died in 1810, leaving her family **in debt**, so Mary began selling her fossils to collectors. A year later, aged just 12, she made her first **major** discovery—a crocodile-like skull[1] with a long skeleton. It turned out to be a sea creature that lived long ago. Named *ichthyosaur*, or "fish-lizard," it was the first extinct animal known to science.

C Fossil hunting brought in money, but it was a dangerous occupation. One day, a rock fall killed her dog and almost buried Mary. Despite the dangers, she **continued** to look for new finds. The long-necked fossil she uncovered in 1823 was another long-dead sea reptile.[2] Known as a *plesiosaur*, it would inspire legends—including that of the Loch Ness Monster. Five years later, she found a fossil with wing bones and a long tail. It was one of the first examples of a *pterosaur*—a flying creature that disappeared millions of years ago.

D Mary was not only a skilled fossil hunter; she also carefully examined and recorded her finds. However, she received little **credit** from other scientists. Only one of her scientific writings was published in her lifetime, in 1839. She was also not allowed to join London's Geological Society, as only men could become members.

E Mary Anning died in 1847, but her **contributions** have not been forgotten. Her finds are now **displayed** in museums in London and Paris. The beach near her home is a UNESCO World Heritage Site, known as the Jurassic Coast. Her life continues to inspire visitors hoping to find their own fossil wonders. According to Britain's Natural History Museum, Mary Anning was "the greatest fossil hunter the world has ever known." She was also a scientist who changed the way we think about life on Earth.

---

1 An animal's **skull** is the part of its skeleton covering its brain.
2 **Reptiles** are cold-blooded animals such as snakes, lizards, and crocodiles.

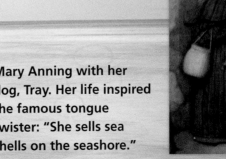

Mary Anning with her dog, Tray. Her life inspired the famous tongue twister: "She sells sea shells on the seashore."

GIANTS
OF THE SKIES

Scientists have been fascinated with pterosaurs ever since their discovery by Mary Anning and other early fossil hunters. These winged reptiles achieved powered flight tens of millions of years before birds or bats. Now scientists are beginning to understand how they did this.

The neck and head together stretched more than six meters.

short neck

sharp teeth

long tail

PTEROSAURS: RISE AND FALL

Pterosaurs ruled the skies for over 160 million years. The earliest were small with long tails; later versions—like *Quetzalcoatlus*—stood as tall as giraffes. Pterosaur fossils have been discovered around the world, mostly in China, Brazil, the United States, Germany, and England.

TRIASSIC

JURASSIC

CRETACEOUS

228 mya

145 mya

PTEROSAURS

Dimorphodon
Wingspan: 1.2 m
Mary Anning discovered the first fossil of this early pterosaur at Lyme Regis in 1828.

Anurognathus ammoni
Wingspan: 60 cm

Tupandactylus navigans
Wingspan: 3 m

BIRDS

DESIGNED FOR FLIGHT

Over millions of years, pterosaurs, bats, and birds adapted the same five arm bones (color-coded here) into three different wing designs.

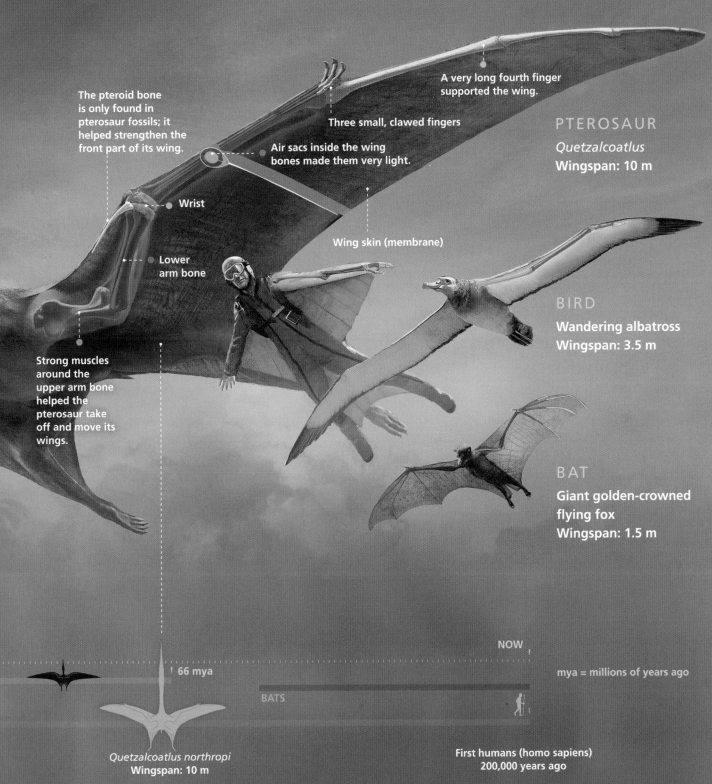

The pteroid bone is only found in pterosaur fossils; it helped strengthen the front part of its wing.

A very long fourth finger supported the wing.

Three small, clawed fingers

Air sacs inside the wing bones made them very light.

Wrist

Lower arm bone

Wing skin (membrane)

Strong muscles around the upper arm bone helped the pterosaur take off and move its wings.

PTEROSAUR
Quetzalcoatlus
Wingspan: 10 m

BIRD
Wandering albatross
Wingspan: 3.5 m

BAT
Giant golden-crowned flying fox
Wingspan: 1.5 m

NOW

66 mya

mya = millions of years ago

BATS

Quetzalcoatlus northropi
Wingspan: 10 m

First humans (homo sapiens)
200,000 years ago

A. Choose the best answer for each question.

GIST

1. What would be the best alternative title for the passage?

a. Long-Necked Creatures from the Past
b. The World's Greatest Fossil Hunter
c. The Discovery of the First Pterosaur

MAIN IDEA

2. Why did Mary Anning start selling fossils?

a. to earn money to support her family
b. to raise public interest in her articles
c. to gain money to start a museum

DETAIL

3. Which of the following is true about Mary Anning?

a. She published several scientific articles in her lifetime.
b. She was nearly killed by a rock fall near the beach.
c. She was a member of the London Geological Society.

DETAIL

4. What is true about the pterosaur find?

a. It looked similar to the Loch Ness Monster.
b. It was the first discovery of an extinct animal.
c. It showed that some extinct creatures had wings.

Dimorphodon **was one of the earliest pterosaurs.**

PURPOSE

5. Why does the author mention a UNESCO World Heritage Site?

a. to persuade the reader that the Jurassic Coast is in need of protection
b. to give an example of how important Mary Anning's discoveries are to the world
c. to show how southern England has the most important fossil finds in the world

CREATING A TIMELINE

B. Add the events (1–5) to complete a timeline of Mary Anning's life.

Review this reading skill in Unit 3A

1. discovers an early pterosaur

2. finds a long-necked fossil

3. makes her first important discovery

4. only scientific writing published

5. starts selling fossils to earn money

1810	1811		1823	1828		1839
☐	☐		☐	☐		☐

1799 •——• 1847
1800   1810   1820   1830   1840

Interpreting Infographics

An information graphic (infographic) uses both text and visuals to present information about a certain topic. It may show many different kinds of information, such as images, diagrams, timelines, as well as text captions and labels. Look for information in keys, and other clues such as use of colors, to help you understand how the parts of the infographic relate to each other.

ANALYZING **A.** What information does the infographic Giants of the Skies show? Check (✓) all that are true.

☐ a. the features of a pterosaur wing that enabled it to fly

☐ b. how arm bones developed in four different animals

☐ c. the relationship between adult pterosaurs and their young

☐ d. how long pterosaurs lived on Earth compared with other animals

ANALYZING **B.** Check (✓) all the statements that are true for each question.

1. Look at the wing labels on the *Quetzalcoatlus*. What helped it fly?

☐ a. a special bone to strengthen the front part of the wing

☐ b. a long finger to support the wing end

☐ c. strong muscles to help with takeoff

☐ d. light feathers to control direction

☐ e. air sacs to reduce bone weight

2. What can we learn from the timeline on the infographic?

☐ a. The first pterosaurs lived more than sixty million years before the first birds.

☐ b. Pterosaurs, birds, and bats all lived on Earth at the same time millions of years ago.

☐ c. *Quetzalcoatlus* was one of the last types of pterosaur to live on Earth.

CRITICAL THINKING Analyzing Claims   The writer claims that Mary Anning was "a scientist who changed the way we think about life on Earth." What evidence is given to support this claim? Note three facts or examples from the passage.

_____

_____

_____

COMPLETION **A.** Complete the information using the words in the box. One item is extra.

continue	credit	displayed	extraordinary	major	noticed	talent

The ¹_____ creature pictured here, *Quetzalcoatlus*, was one of the largest flying animals of all time. An American graduate student, Douglas A. Lawson, is given ²_____ for its discovery in 1971. One day, Lawson ³_____ a large wing bone on the ground during a visit to Big Bend National Park in Texas. Since then, only a few remains have been found, but scientists ⁴_____ to look for more. This life-size model will be ⁵_____ in Sheikh Jaber Al Ahmad Cultural Center, a ⁶_____ new museum project in Kuwait.

∧ *Quetzalcoatlus northropi* was a giant pterosaur.

DEFINITIONS **B.** Complete the definitions. Circle the correct options.

1. Someone who has **debt**, or is **in debt**, *needs to pay back / wants to give out* money to other people.

2. If you make a **contribution** to something, you *help with it / make it more difficult*.

3. Someone with a lot of **talent** *hopes / is able* to do something very well.

4. If you **arrange** objects, you place them in a *hidden location / particular position*.

WORD FORMS **C.** Some words, like **notice** and **credit**, can act as nouns and verbs.

Example: Did you **notice** the unusual rocks along the coastline?
The **notice** says we're not allowed to enter the beach.

Choose two words from the box. Write two sentences using each one, first as a noun and then as a verb.

find	record	rescue	spot	store

_____

_____

BEFORE YOU READ

DEFINITIONS **A.** Read the photo caption below. Match each word in **bold** with its definition.

1. _____ (n) an organized trip with a specific purpose
2. _____ (n) animals that hunt and eat other animals
3. _____ (n) people who study fossils

SKIMMING **B.** Skim the reading passage. Find at least two things that Jørn Hurum has in common with Mary Anning.

Review this reading skill in Unit 1A

⌃ A group of **paleontologists** search for fossils during an **expedition** to Svalbard—a group of islands in the Arctic Ocean. The fossils of a number of huge prehistoric sea **predators** have been discovered in the area, preserved in the rock for more than 150 million years.

THE STORIES
IN THE ROCKS

^ Jørn Hurum
on expedition

A When he was just six years old, Jørn Hurum turned his bedroom into a small museum. His shelves became filled with a growing **collection** of fossils. For Hurum, these fossils were not just rocks, but things that could tell the history of life on this planet. He imagined them saying, "I am not a rock. I am a fossil. I have a story to tell."

B Hurum earned a PhD in paleontology in his native Norway. Since then, he has been on expeditions seeking fossils all over the world. Much of his work has been carried out in Svalbard, a group of Norwegian islands north of the Arctic Circle. In the hills of this cold and **remote** region, Hurum and his team have found the fossils of many sea creatures. It might seem surprising to find the remains[1] of such animals at the tops of hills, but in prehistoric times, these areas were actually seabeds about 100 meters deep.

C Hurum has returned to Svalbard many times. The "dig season" in the region is very short—from July to August. During that time, the temperature is just about warm enough to **soften** the frozen ground, allowing easier **access** to the fossils. There is also less wind, and the "midnight sun" makes it easy for the scientists to have long, **productive** days.

D Even a dream job has its challenges, however. "Sometimes, we find 'explodasaurus,'" he says. The team may find many broken bone pieces spread across a hillside. Then it becomes impossible to recreate the entire animal: "We have to identify the **entire** animal from **individual** pieces." Each of Hurum's expeditions also requires a lot of **preparation**. "We have between 15 and 20 people, tons of equipment—food, jackhammers,[2] water," he explains. "There's a lot of work before you start the cool thing."

E For Hurum, the "cool thing," is the act of discovery. In 2006, his team made its greatest discovery so far. After **removing** about 60 tons of rock by hand, Hurum and his team **eventually** dug out an enormous fossil. "We knew immediately this was something special," says Hurum. "The large pieces of bone … told us that this was big." It was a plesiosaur—a prehistoric sea monster with teeth the size of cucumbers. The fossil was not complete, but it included a front flipper, a shoulder, and pieces of skull and neck.

F For Hurum, the discovery of this 15-meter-long creature— nicknamed "Predator X"—was an amazing moment. "It's like one of those scratch-off lottery tickets every time you dig," he explains. "Sometimes, you start digging and you might just find part of a skull or other bone. Sometimes, you find the skull and the vertebra … Then you know it's a jackpot!"

---

1 The **remains** of something are the parts of it that are left once it has been destroyed or taken away.
2 **Jackhammers** are large tools used for breaking up rocks.

A. Choose the best answer for each question.

GIST

1. What is the reading mainly about?

    a. a paleontologist who followed his dream from a young age

    b. the best areas in the world to find fossils of sea creatures

    c. the discovery of the largest plesiosaur ever found

DETAIL

2. In Svalbard, where does Hurum find most fossils?

    a. on the hills

    b. at the bottom of lakes and rivers

    c. on beaches near the sea

DETAIL

3. Which of the following is NOT mentioned as a reason why July to August is the best time to search for fossils in Svalbard?

    a. The ground is softer than usual.

    b. There are long hours of daylight.

    c. There is regular transport to the area.

∧ **Jørn Hurum**

INFERENCE

4. What is Hurum referring to when he mentions "explodasaurus"?

    a. a species of dinosaur that he wants to discover

    b. the fossil of Predator X

    c. fossils that are found in many pieces

INFERENCE

5. Why does Hurum mention "scratch-off lottery tickets"?

    a. to give an example of how much money the expeditions cost

    b. to describe how lucky he feels to work as a paleontologist

    c. to explain that you need luck to find the most amazing discoveries

SCANNING

Review this reading skill in Unit 2B

B. Write short answers to the questions below. Use 2–3 words from the passage for each answer.

1. How did the paleontologists remove the rock surrounding the Predator X fossil?

_____

2. Where was the museum that Hurum created when he was a child?

_____

3. What name is used to refer to the period in Svalbard from July to August?

_____

4. What three examples of expedition equipment does Hurum mention?

_____

Dealing with Unfamiliar Vocabulary (2)—Affixes

Affixes are word parts that are added to a word's base form to modify its meaning or to create a new word. Understanding the meaning of certain affixes can help you guess the meaning of unfamiliar vocabulary as you read. There are two types of affix: **prefixes** (at the beginning of a word) and **suffixes** (at the end of a word). Here are some examples with their usual meanings:

Prefix	Example	Suffix	Example
un- = not	*unfriendly*	**-en** = cause to be	*widen*
over- = too much	*overcook*	**-er / -or / -ist** = one who	*worker*
pre- = before	*preview*	**-ful** = full of	*fearful*
re- = again, back	*replace*	**-ion / -tion** = act or process	*attraction*

DEFINITIONS   **A.** In each sentence from Reading B, underline the word that contains a prefix or suffix from the box above. Then write a short definition for the underlined word.

Example: He had wanted to be a <u>paleontologist</u> from a very young age.
Definition: (n) *someone who studies fossils*

1. ... in prehistoric times, these areas were actually seabeds ...

Definition: _____

2. When he was just six years old, Hurum had his own collection of fossils ...

Definition: _____

3. There is also less wind, and the "midnight sun" makes it easy for the scientists ...

Definition: _____

4. During that time, the temperature is just about warm enough to soften the ... ground.

Definition: _____

SCANNING   **B.** Look back at Reading A. Find and write a word that contains each prefix or suffix below. Then write a sentence with each word.

1. un- (paragraph A) _____   **3.** -er (paragraph D) _____

2. un- (paragraph B) _____   **4.** -or (paragraph E) _____

_____

_____

_____

_____

COMPLETION **A.** Complete the information using the words in the box. Two words are extra.

access (n)	collection	entire	eventually
individual	preparation	productive	remote

Plesiosaurs were a species of prehistoric marine reptile. They first appeared about 203 million years ago and became especially common during the Jurassic Period. They lived in oceans throughout the ¹_____ world, thriving until they ²_____ disappeared at the end of the Cretaceous Period, about 66 million years ago.

Plesiosaurs were discovered in the beginning of the 19th century, and since then, efforts to learn more about these creatures have been hugely ³_____. Many more discoveries have provided scientists with a large ⁴_____ of plesiosaur fossils to study, and more than a hundred ⁵_____ species have now been described. With ⁶_____ to so many specimens, paleontologists now have a fairly complete idea of what these amazing animals looked like.

COMPLETION **B.** Complete the sentences. Circle the correct words.

1. Paleontologists need to do a lot of **preparation** / **collection** before going on an expedition.

2. Fossils are often found in **remote** / **entire** regions of the world.

3. Special equipment is needed to **remote** / **remove** large fossils from the ground.

4. Rather than trying to recover a fossil in freezing conditions, it's best to wait until the temperature rises and the ground **removes** / **softens**.

COLLOCATIONS **C.** The verbs in the box are frequently used with the noun **access**. Complete the sentences using the correct form of the words.

deny	gain	provide

1. The new road will _____ easier access to the region's national park.

2. The hackers were able to _____ access to the customers' bank account details in just a few minutes.

3. I was _____ access to the website because I had forgotten my password.

DIGGING INTO THE PAST

Scientist Aubrey Jane Roberts uncovers a fossil in Spitsbergen, Norway.

BEFORE YOU WATCH

DEFINITIONS **A.** The words in **bold** appear in the video. Complete the definitions by circling the correct options.

1. A **marine** reptile is an animal such as a snake or lizard that lives *in the sea / on land*.

2. If you have a **passion** for something, you really *don't like / like* it.

3. **Backbreaking** work involves *a lot of / very little* physical effort.

PREVIEWING **B.** Look at the information about Aubrey Roberts below that appears in the video. What words do you think complete the text? Discuss your ideas with a partner.

Name: Aubrey Jane Roberts   **Job:** P_____

Location: Spitsbergen, Norway

Objective: Uncover 250-million-year-old marine reptile b_____.

Qualifications: Ability to d_____ o_____ 40 tons of earth.

Requirements: Love d_____, digging, and demolition.

GIST **A.** Watch the video. Check your predictions in Before You Watch B.

MULTIPLE CHOICE **B.** Watch the video again. Choose the correct answer for each question.

1. What would be a suitable alternative title for the video?

   a. How to Become a Fossil Hunter

   b. The Dream Job of a Dinosaur Lover

2. Why did people think Roberts was unusual as a child?

   a. because she had a great passion for dinosaurs

   b. because she loved going on outdoor adventures

3. According to Roberts, what part of the job "makes your heart leap"?

   a. discovering something under a rock

   b. seeing the amazing scenery for the first time

4. What does Roberts say she loves about paleontology?

   a. Any new discovery involves a lot of teamwork.

   b. New discoveries are being made all the time.

CRITICAL THINKING Ranking Items   Imagine you are a member of a fossil-hunting expedition heading to Svalbard. Which of the following items do you think will be most useful to take with you? Check (✓) the five most useful items. Share the reasons for your choices with a partner.

☐ a fishing kit   ☐ a gun   ☐ a jackhammer

☐ a small radio   ☐ a map of Svalbard   ☐ a magnifying glass

☐ a medical kit   ☐ a smart phone   ☐ a 5 × 5 meter plastic sheet

VOCABULARY REVIEW

Do you remember the meanings of these words? Check (✓) the ones you know. Look back at the unit and review any words you're not sure of.

Reading A

☐ arrange   ☐ continue   ☐ contribution*   ☐ credit*   ☐ debt

☐ display*   ☐ extraordinary   ☐ major*   ☐ notice   ☐ talent

Reading B

☐ access*   ☐ collection   ☐ entire   ☐ eventually*   ☐ individual*

☐ preparation   ☐ productive   ☐ remote   ☐ remove*   ☐ soften

* Academic Word List

6

REEF
ENCOUNTERS

A spine-cheek clownfish
hides in a sea anemone on
a coral reef.

WARM UP

Discuss these questions
with a partner.

1. What do you know about
    coral reefs? Can you think
    of any famous ones?

2. What are some threats to
    the world's oceans?

BEFORE YOU READ

TRUE OR FALSE   **A.** Look at the picture and read the caption. Are the sentences below true or false? Circle **T** (true) or **F** (false).

1. Coral reefs are usually found in warm water.   **T**   F
2. Coral polyps are a type of plant.   T   **F**
3. A coral reef usually gets smaller over time.   T   **F**
4. Some coral reefs are over a million years old   **T**   F

PREDICTING   **B.** Look quickly at the title, headings, photos, and captions on the following pages. Check (✓) the information you think you will read about. Then read the passage to check your ideas.

☐ how coral reefs are formed   ☐ problems affecting reefs
☐ coral reef wildlife   ☐ threats to coral fishermen

CITIES
BENEATH THE SEA

A For uncounted generations, trillions[1] upon trillions of coral polyps have lived and died, leaving behind a material called limestone. Prized throughout history, limestone was used to **construct** the Great Pyramids of Egypt, as well as many churches and castles. Yet the greatest limestone structures in the world are built underwater, by the coral polyps themselves. We call them reefs. They can be even larger in scale than the most impressive buildings and structures made by humans.

1 A **trillion** is 1,000,000,000,000.

A Variety of Life

B Indeed, a living coral reef is **remarkable**, a "city beneath the sea" filled with a rich variety of life. Most coral reefs can be found in warm, **shallow** oceans. They **occupy** just a small part of the ocean floor, but host 25 percent of all ocean life.

C Coral reefs display nature's most **brilliant** colors. Each reef is full of colorful fish as well as coral that form wonderful patterns. In addition to their beauty, the reefs are an important food source for fish, and for humans. In fact, reef fish make up a significant percentage of the global fish catch.

< Mostly found in water warmed by sunlight, reefs are built by coral polyps—tiny, soft-bodied animals related to jellyfish. As more coral polyps come together, the reef grows. Some coral reefs began growing over 50 million years ago.

RESIDENTS OF THE REEF

Coral reefs occupy less than 1 percent of the surface area of the world's oceans, but they provide a home for 25 percent of all marine fish species. Here are some examples of the creatures that call a coral reef home.

⌄ Spot-banded butterflyfish

⌃ A blue-girdled angelfish

⌄ A redfin butterflyfish

▽ A nudibranch uses its bright colors to tell predators to stay away.

▽ A longsnout seahorse "stands" between coral branches.

▽ A red jellyfish swims above a coral reef in the Philippines.

Threats to Coral Reefs

D Various human activities can cause great harm to the world's coral reefs. For example, reefs can be damaged when the coral is taken for use in building materials, jewelry-making, or to fill aquariums.[2]

E Illegal fishing methods like blast and cyanide fishing also harm the reefs. These methods can help fishermen get a good catch, but their **negative** effects on the reefs are significant. Blast fishing involves setting off bombs in the water to kill as many fish as possible. This kills most living things nearby and causes damage to the reef's structure.

F In cyanide fishing, fishermen **release** liquid cyanide—a very dangerous and deadly **chemical**—into the reef. As a result, the fish become stunned,[3] which makes them easy to collect. Meanwhile, the reef is damaged by the cyanide, which kills large numbers of coral polyps. The reef is also damaged by the fishermen who break it apart looking for the stunned fish.

G Another threat is water **pollution**. When floods[4] in Australia covered the Great Barrier Reef with dirty freshwater, the quality of the water changed and chemicals killed the reef life. This is happening to many reefs around the world.

H In addition, global warming has caused many reefs to become sick. Warmer temperatures have turned them white, in a process known as coral bleaching. A 2018 UN Report predicted that up to 99 percent of the world's coral reefs may decline if global warming continues.

Reasons for Hope

I These threats to coral reefs are very serious, but there is reason to hope that they will survive. If we take steps toward coral reef **conservation**, it is likely that these tiny creatures—which survived natural threats for millions of years—will be able to rebuild. As conservationist Robert Richmond says, "Given a chance, they can come back."

---

2 An **aquarium** is a tank or building where sea animals are kept.

3 If an animal is **stunned**, it is confused or hurt and unable to move.

4 A **flood** is a large amount of water covering an area of land that is usually dry.

A. Choose the best answer for each question.

GIST

1. What is the reading mainly about?

a. efforts to save the world's coral reefs

b. the kinds of animals found near coral reefs

c. the beauty of reefs and the dangers they face

DETAIL

2. Which statement about coral reefs is NOT true?

a. They are usually found in deep ocean waters.

b. They are among the world's most colorful places.

c. They can be larger than structures made by humans.

▲ **A coral polyp**

DETAIL

3. Why do some fishermen use the method of blast fishing?

a. to destroy the coral reefs

b. to kill as many fish as possible

c. to stun the fish and make them easier to catch

PARAPHRASING

4. What was the conclusion of the 2018 UN Report mentioned in paragraph H?

a. If global temperatures keep rising, almost all of the world's coral reefs could decline.

b. Global temperatures will continue to rise, and this may cause more coral bleaching.

c. The bleaching of coral reefs is likely to increase the speed of global warming.

MAIN IDEA

5. Which sentence best expresses the main idea of the final paragraph?

a. Governments around the world are working to save coral reefs.

b. There is hope because conservationists have already saved many reefs.

c. With our help, coral reefs can continue to survive.

UNDERSTANDING AFFIXES

Review this reading skill in Unit 5B

B. In each sentence from the reading, write a definition for the **bold** word.

1. For **uncounted** generations, trillions upon trillions of coral … (paragraph A)

Definition: _no able to count_

2. Each reef is full of **colorful** fish … (paragraph C)

Definition: _lots of color_

3. … these tiny creatures … will be able to **rebuild** … (paragraph I)

Definition: _build again_

Understanding Cause-and-Effect Relationships

Understanding cause-and-effect relationships within a text is an important part of reading comprehension.

A *cause* is an action that makes something happen. An *effect* is a result of that action. Certain connecting words show these relationships. In these examples, the cause is *the heavy rain* and the effect is *the flood.*

The heavy rain **caused / resulted in / was the reason for** *the flood.*

There was heavy rain. **Therefore, / Consequently, / As a result,** *there was a flood.*

There was heavy rain, **so** *there was a flood.*

Because of / As a result of *the heavy rain, there was a flood.*

To improve your understanding of certain texts, it can be useful to summarize any cause-and-effect relationships in a chart.

IDENTIFYING CAUSES AND EFFECTS

A. Circle the causes and underline the effects in this text.

Not all reefs begin naturally. For example, an ocean current may encounter a man-made object, like a sunken ship. As a result, the water around the ship may become rich with tiny animals called plankton. A lot of small fish gather there to feed on the plankton. Consequently, larger animals are attracted to the ship. Because the ship has many little openings, many creatures also have a place to hide. In time, the ship becomes covered in polyps. As a result, it no longer looks like a ship at all.

UNDERSTANDING CAUSES AND EFFECTS

B. Use the information in activity A to complete the chart.

Causes	Effects
1. Ocean current encounters sunken ship.	The water rich with Plankton
2. A lot of small fish gather there to feed.	Larger animals are atracted to the ship
3. The ship has many openings →	Many creatures have a place to hide.
4. The ship becomes covered in polyps	It doesn't look like a ship

CRITICAL THINKING Evaluating Ideas   Look at the suggestions for protecting coral reefs. Rank them 1–4 (1 = the best idea). Discuss your ideas with a partner and explain your reasons.

_4_ ban all fishing near coral reefs   _3_ ban people from selling coral products

_2_ stop tourists from diving near reefs   _1_ start a campaign to raise awareness

DEFINITIONS **A.** Read the information. Then match each word in **red** with its definition.

Not all coral is found in warm, **shallow** water. Some coral polyps can survive in cold water at the bottom of the ocean. But even there, they're not safe. Fishing boats— called bottom trawlers—pull heavy nets across the ocean floor. These nets have a very **negative** effect on deep sea coral and the **remarkable** sea life around it. Because the **conservation** of these corals is important, the United States has a law that prevents bottom trawling in over a million square kilometers of ocean off its Pacific coast.

1. harmful or bad _negative_
2. the opposite of *deep* _shallow_
3. special and amazing _remarkable_
4. taking care of the environment _conservation_

▲ **A heavy net is dragged across the ocean floor by a bottom trawler.**

WORDS IN CONTEXT

B. Complete the sentences. Circle the correct options.

1. If you catch a fish and then **release** it, you *don't keep /* (*keep* it.)
2. If you **construct** a house, you (*build*) / *buy* it.
3. If you **occupy** a place, you (*stay*) / *leave* there.
4. In a city with high levels of **pollution**, the air is likely to be very *clean* / (*dirty*).
5. A color that is described as **brilliant** is probably very (*bright*) / *dark*.
6. People often create **chemicals** in a *library* / (*science lab*).

COLLOCATIONS

C. The nouns in the box are often used with the word **negative**. Complete the sentences with the correct form of the words in the box.

effect	meaning	response	thought

1. The word *skinny* has a more negative _thought_ than the word *slim*.
2. There was a largely negative _effect_ / _response_ to the government's plans to increase income tax.
3. Playing video games late at night can have a negative _meaning_ / _effect_ on your sleep.
4. Sports psychologists believe that negative _meaning_ / _thought_ can affect an athlete's performance.

BEFORE YOU READ

QUIZ **A.** Do you think the following statements about great white sharks are true or false? Circle **T** (true) or **F** (false). Discuss your ideas with a partner.

   1. Most shark attacks are by great white sharks.   **T**   **F**

   2. Most people do not survive an attack by a great white shark. **T**   **F**

   3. There is more chance of being killed by lightning   **T**   **F**
   than by a great white shark.

   4. Great white sharks have around 300 teeth.   **T**   **F**

SKIMMING **B.** Skim the passage and check your ideas in activity A.

Great white sharks attack
their prey at speeds of up to
40 kilometers an hour.

> Divers in the Caribbean Sea study a large great white shark from the safety of their diving cage.

THE TRUTH
ABOUT GREAT WHITES

A In sunny California, Craig Rogers was sitting on his surfboard,[1] scanning the distance for his next wave. Suddenly, his board stopped moving. He looked down and was terrified to see a great white shark **biting** the front of his board. "I could have touched its eye with my elbow," says Rogers. The shark had surfaced so quietly that he didn't hear a thing. In his **horror** and **confusion**, he waved his arms and accidentally cut two of his fingers on the shark's teeth. He got off the opposite side of his surfboard, into the water. Then, despite Rogers being in the water with blood **flowing** from his fingers, the five-meter-long shark simply swam away.

B Over a hundred shark attacks happen worldwide each year. Of these, one-third are said to be great white attacks. Great whites are often described as "man-eaters"—creatures that hunt and kill humans—but this is factually **inaccurate**. Great whites rarely kill their human **victims**. In fact, a person has a greater chance of being killed by lightning[2] than by a great white. With **frightening** jaws that hold around 300 teeth in several rows, a great white can kill very easily. Surprisingly though, most great white victims live to tell the tale. Shark researchers are trying to understand the reasons great whites attack people, and why most of those people manage to escape a horrible death.

> ⌄ Great whites can be found in seas all over the world. In some places, such as Australia and South Africa, they are protected.

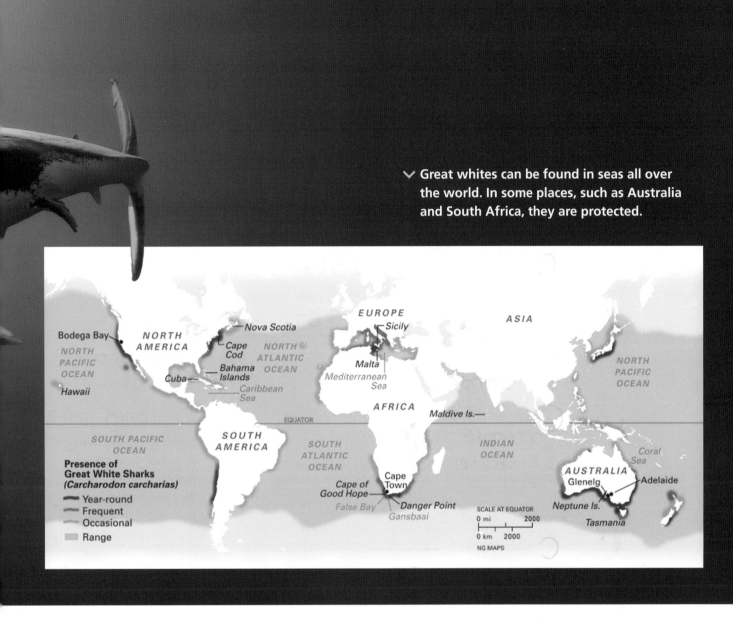

C One of the most common explanations for great white attacks is that great whites don't see well. It is thought that they often mistake a person for a seal or sea lion—a very **tempting** snack. However, there is reason to doubt this. Some research now shows that great whites can actually see—and identify seals—very well. When attacking seals, great whites shoot up to the surface and bite with great **force**. However, when they approach humans, they often move in slowly and bite with less force. "They take a bite, feel them over, then move on," says Peter Klimley, author of *The Secret Lives of Sharks*.

D Shark experts like Klimley believe that great whites "attack" because they are actually curious animals that like to investigate things. They believe that it's possible great whites use their bite not just to kill and eat, but also to **gather** information. According to this idea, once a great white identifies what it is biting, it simply lets go.

E Even though such experiences are unlucky for people like Craig Rogers, perhaps when sharks bite surfboards, other objects, or even people, they are just trying to learn what they are.

---

1 A **surfboard** is a long, narrow board used for surfing.
2 The bright flashes of light and electricity often seen in the sky during rainstorms is **lightning**.

A. Choose the best answer for each question.

GIST

1. What would be the best alternative title for the reading?

    a. How to Survive a Shark Attack

    b. Why Great Whites Kill Humans

    c. Great Whites: Facts and Fiction

DETAIL

2. After Craig Rogers fell into the water, ___.

    a. the shark swam away

    b. the shark bit his fingers

    c. the shark bit his surfboard

PURPOSE

3. What is the purpose of paragraph C?

    a. to explain why great whites don't see well

    b. to provide advice on what to do if you see a great white

    c. to give possible reasons why great whites don't kill humans

REFERENCE

4. In the last sentence of paragraph C, the word *them* refers to ___.

    a. people

    b. teeth

    c. great whites

FACT OR SPECULATION?

5. Which statement is a fact and not speculation?

    a. Great whites are not able to see well.

    b. Great whites bite to get information.

    c. Great whites eat seals and sea lions.

▲ **A great white shark tooth (pictured here in actual size) can measure more than six centimeters long.**

UNDERSTANDING MAPS AND INFOGRAPHICS

Review this reading skill in Unit 5A

B. Look at the map on the previous page. Complete each sentence (1–3) with the correct ending (a–d). One ending is extra.

    a. off the coasts of countries close to the equator

    b. off the southern coast of Tasmania

    c. off the southern coasts of Australia and South Africa

    d. in the cold waters near the North and South Poles

1. Great white sharks can be found all year round __c__.

2. There are no great white sharks __d__.

3. Great white sharks are only occasionally found __a__.

Recognizing Contrastive Relationships

Writers use certain words and phrases to indicate a contrast between ideas presented in a text. It is important to identify and understand these phrases in order to fully comprehend the passage. The words and phrases in **bold** below are common examples.

I'm a good swimmer, **but** / **yet** _I rarely go swimming._

I'm a good swimmer. **However,** _I rarely go swimming._

Though / **Although** / **Even though** _I'm afraid of the water,_ I went swimming.

I went swimming **though** / **although** / **even though** _I'm afraid of the water._

I went swimming in the sea **despite** / **in spite of** _the bad weather._

Despite / **In spite of** _the bad weather,_ I went swimming in the sea.

RECOGNIZING CONTRAST

A. These sentences are from the reading. Circle the correct connecting words. Look back at Reading B to check your answers.

1. Then, **but** / **despite** Rogers being in the water with blood flowing from his fingers, the five-meter-long shark simply swam away.

2. A great white can very easily kill. Surprisingly, **although** / **though**, most great white victims live to tell the tale.

3. It is thought that they often mistake a person for a seal or a sea lion—a very tempting snack. **However** / **Even though**, there is reason to doubt this.

4. **Even though** / **However** such experiences are unlucky for people like Craig Rogers, perhaps when sharks bite surfboards, other objects, or even people, they are just trying to learn what they are.

UNDERSTANDING CONTRAST

B. Combine each pair of sentences using the word or phrase in parentheses.

1. Great white sharks are dangerous. They rarely kill humans. (**even though**)

   _____

2. Great white sharks are often seen off the coast of Australia. Surfing is popular there. (**however**)

   _____

CRITICAL THINKING Analyzing Reasons

▶ Look back at paragraphs C and D of the reading. What are the two explanations for great white shark attacks that the author mentions? Note your answers below.

   _____

▶ Which explanation does the author think is more likely? How do you know? Discuss with a partner.

COMPLETION **A.** Complete the information with words from the box. One word is extra.

> bite confusion flow horror inaccurate victims

In 1974, writer Peter Benchley wrote the famous novel *Jaws,* about a killer shark that hunts its human ¹ _victims_. The next year, Steven Spielberg made a movie of the same name. While the movie was popular, it led to some ² _confusion_ about the true nature of great whites. The movie made the great white into a symbol of ³ _horror_ and death. However, the behavior of the shark shown in *Jaws* is actually ⁴ _inaccurate_. The truth is that great whites rarely ⁵ _bite_ humans. Years later, Benchley and Spielberg both felt bad about creating a false image of these creatures.

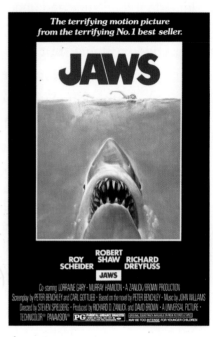

The terrifying motion picture from the terrifying No. 1 best seller.

JAWS

ROY SCHEIDER ROBERT SHAW RICHARD DREYFUSS

JAWS

Co-starring LORRAINE GARY · MURRAY HAMILTON · A ZANUCK/BROWN PRODUCTION
Screenplay by PETER BENCHLEY and CARL GOTTLIEB · Based on the novel by PETER BENCHLEY · Music by JOHN WILLIAMS
Directed by STEVEN SPIELBERG · Produced by RICHARD D. ZANUCK and DAVID BROWN · A UNIVERSAL PICTURE ·
TECHNICOLOR® PANAVISION® · PG PARENTAL GUIDANCE SUGGESTED   ORIGINAL SOUNDTRACK AVAILABLE ON MCA RECORDS & TAPES   MAY BE TOO INTENSE FOR YOUNGER CHILDREN

WORDS IN CONTEXT **B.** Choose the correct words to complete the sentences.

1. Most but not all rivers **flow** / force into the sea.

2. Seeing a shark in the water is a **frightening** / tempting experience.

3. Shark researchers often put food in the ocean. Its **tempting** / gathering smell attracts the sharks.

4. Serious damage from a shark bite is due to the size and sharpness of its teeth, rather than the flow / **force** of its bite.

5. Each year, great white sharks **gather** / flow near Cape Town to eat seals, which are plentiful in South Africa's water.

WORD PARTS **C.** The word **inaccurate** is formed using the prefix *in-*. The prefix can be added to other words to make their opposite. Complete the sentences with the words in the box.

> complete correct expensive

1. Though scientists know a lot about sharks, their knowledge is still in_complete_.

2. The idea that sharks are man-eaters is largely in_correct_.

3. Scientists are looking for new, in_expensive_ ways of collecting data about sharks.

˅ **A small airplane flies above Australia's Great Barrier Reef.**

OCEAN MEGABUILDERS

BEFORE YOU WATCH

PREVIEWING **A.** Read the information. The words in **bold** appear in the video. Match each word with its definition.

Located off the coast of Australia, the Great Barrier Reef Marine Park **stretches** for over 3,000 kilometers. It provides a **habitat** for thousands of diverse species of sea creatures. All these creatures depend on the coral polyp **colonies** that make up the reef. Sadly, in 2016, scientists found that 30 percent of the reef's corals died as a result of a heatwave. Today, scientists **warn** that it may be too late to save much of the reef and its beautiful coral, but they are trying to find ways to stop the damage.

1. habitat   a. (v) to tell someone about possible danger
2. colony   b. (n) a place where something can live
3. warn   c. (v) to cover an area or distance
4. stretch   d. (n) a large group of individuals that live in the same place

QUIZ **B.** What do you remember about coral reefs from Reading A? Discuss the questions below with a partner.

1. Are coral reefs mainly found in warm or cool waters around the world?
2. What is the name of the tiny creatures that make up coral reefs? *Polyp*
3. What material is used in the building of coral reefs? *limestone*

GIST **A.** Watch the video. Check your answers in Before You Watch B.

COMPLETION **B.** Read the notes below. Complete the information as you watch the video again.

Coral Reef Facts:

- A reef is made up of animals called polyps. Biggest polyps are the size of a
  1 basketball

- The Great Barrier Reef is the 2 oldest coral reef in the world. It is around
  3 50,000 years old.

- Coral reefs provide habitats for 4 25% percent of all sea creatures.

- By studying limestone layers, scientists learn about the Earth's past 5 weather.

- About 6 500 million people depend on fish that live on coral reefs.

- Scientists think that without action, many reefs will disappear by 7 end of 21st
  century

CRITICAL THINKING Evaluating Sources   Consider what you have learned about coral reefs in this unit. Which source, the reading or the video, best helped you understand the following? Why?

how coral reefs are formed   the threats facing coral reefs

why coral reefs are important   what we can do to protect coral reefs

VOCABULARY REVIEW

Do you remember the meanings of these words? Check (✓) the ones you know. Look back at the unit and review any words you're not sure of.

Reading A

☐ brilliant   ☐ chemical*   ☐ conservation   ☐ construct*   ☐ negative*

☐ occupy   ☐ pollution   ☐ release*   ☐ remarkable   ☐ shallow

Reading B

☐ bite   ☐ confusion   ☐ flow   ☐ force   ☐ frightening

☐ gather   ☐ horror   ☐ inaccurate*   ☐ tempting   ☐ victim

* Academic Word List

7

DOLLARS AND SCENTS

A cape marguerite flower. The purpose of a flower's aroma is to attract insects, but humans also find the scents appealing.

WARM UP

Discuss these questions with a partner.

1. How many kinds of flowers can you name in English? Make a list.

2. Which flower do you think is the most beautiful?

BEFORE YOU READ

DEFINITIONS **A.** Match each word or phrase with its definition.

1. cut flowers • • a. a container to hold flowers
2. fragrance • • b. a nice smell
3. vase • • c. a person or a store that sells flowers
4. florist • • d. flowers that are taken off the plant

SCANNING **B.** Do you know any countries that are famous for producing flowers? Discuss your ideas with a partner. Then scan the passage for country names to check your ideas.

Review this Reading Skill in Unit 2B

THE FLOWER
TRADE

A When you purchase fresh-cut flowers, do you think about where they came from? You might **assume** they were grown somewhere nearby. The reality, though, is that the cut flower trade is increasingly international. Today, thanks to airplanes and high-tech cooling systems, even the most delicate[1] flower can be **exported** and sold in a florist thousands of kilometers from where it was grown.

The Cut Flower Leader

B The Netherlands has **dominated** the world cut flower trade since the 1970s. It **handles** about 50 percent of the world's cut flowers. And its auction houses[2] are very large indeed— Aalsmeer, near Amsterdam, is an auction house in the sense that Tokyo is a city. About 120 soccer fields would fill its main building. Twenty million flowers are sold here on an average day, including roses, lilies, and—of course—tulips.

C The Netherlands is also a world leader in developing new flower varieties. Dutch companies and the government **invest** a **considerable** amount of money in flower research. Their scientists look for ways to lengthen a flower's vase life,[3] to strengthen flowers to **prevent** them from being damaged while traveling, and also to strengthen the flowers' natural fragrance.

---

1 Something **delicate** is easy to damage and needs to be treated carefully.
2 **Auction houses** sell items to the customers who offer the highest price.
3 **Vase life** means the amount of time a cut flower remains in good condition.

Netherlands

⟨ **Aalsmeer, the heart of the global flower trade, processes 20 million flowers every day.**

The Benefits of Climate

D Despite the Netherlands' dominance of the flower market, there are many places with a better climate for growing flowers. The climate of Ecuador, for example, is almost perfect. Mauricio Dávalos is the man responsible for starting Ecuador's flower industry, which has grown quickly over recent years. "Our biggest edge is nature," he **claims**. "Our roses are the best in the world." With **predictable** rainy periods and 12 hours of sunlight each day, Ecuador's roses are known for their large heads and long, straight stems. Every year, Ecuador sells about 500 million flowers to the United States alone. The **industry** has brought employment opportunities and a stronger economy to regions of the country. "My family has TV now. There are radios," says Yolanda Quishpe, 20, who picked roses for four years.

E To others, the increasingly international nature of the flower trade is very bad news. In recent years, local growers in the United States faced huge competition from international flower companies; many have even lost their businesses. Lina Hale, an independent rose grower in California, said her father predicted the situation in the 1980s. "I see a freight train coming down the track," he warned her, "and it's coming straight towards us." Her father's prediction—sadly—has largely come true. In a globalized world, what happens in one place often has far-reaching effects.

⌄ **At Aalsmeer, delicate orchid plants are prepared for auction.**

FROM COLOMBIA TO THE UNITED STATES

How a rose travels from mountain to vase in just three days

Tuesday, 7 A.M.

Roses are cut in the cool mountain air of Colombia and moved quickly to indoor cooling houses.

Tuesday, 1 P.M.

Workers categorize the roses based on size, stem length, shape, and color.

Wednesday, 6 A.M.

Roses are boxed and sent to Bogotá Airport for the 3.5-hour flight to Miami.

Wednesday, 8 P.M.

Roses are checked by officials, and then transported by truck, train, or plane.

Thursday, 4 P.M.

Roses arrive at large markets in major U.S. cities, where they are purchased by flower sellers.

READING COMPREHENSION

A. Choose the best answer for each question.

MAIN IDEA

1. What is the main idea of the first paragraph?
   a. Many local florists are disappearing due to competition from large companies in other countries.
   b. The international flower trade has grown a lot in recent years thanks to new technology.
   c. Most people don't realize that the flowers they buy often come from far away.

DETAIL

2. Which statement about Aalsmeer auction house is true?
   a. It processes over half of the world's cut flowers.
   b. It is the size of a large city.
   c. It sells around 20 million flowers each day.

Hybrid teas are the world's most popular variety of rose.

MAIN IDEA

3. According to paragraph D, Ecuador's flower industry _____.
   a. has found it difficult to compete with the United States
   b. has grown quickly due to Ecuador's ideal climate
   c. has been an industry leader since the 1970s

INFERENCE

4. What did Lina Hale's father mean when he said, *I see a freight train coming down the track* (paragraph E)?
   a. He knew his business would be threatened.
   b. He thought customers wouldn't want roses.
   c. He thought trains were the new way to move flowers.

PURPOSE

5. What is the purpose of the "From Colombia to the United States" section?
   a. to show how the international cut flower trade works
   b. to give reasons why Colombian roses are expensive
   c. to explain why Colombian roses always look fresh

SCANNING

Review this reading skill in Unit 2B

B. Write short answers to the questions below. Use two or three words from the passage for each answer.

1. Apart from airplanes, what other technology has helped the flower trade become increasingly international?
   High tech oiling system

2. What phrase describes the length of time a cut flower can stay in good condition?
   Vose life

3. How many flowers are sold on an average day at Aalsmeer auction house?
   20 million

4. What is Lina Hale's job?
   Independet rose grower

Summarizing Using a Venn Diagram

For certain reading passages, it can be useful to summarize information using a Venn diagram. A Venn diagram provides a way of comparing two or more things and presenting similarities and differences visually.

SUMMARIZING **A.** Look back at Reading A. Complete the Venn diagram comparing the flower industries of Ecuador and the Netherlands using the information (a–f).

a. grows roses

b. has dominated the flower market for many years

c. has an ideal climate for growing flowers

d. is a world leader in developing flower varieties

e. is known for producing roses with large heads and straight stems

f. has seen its flower industry grow quickly in recent times

the Netherlands   Both   Ecuador

SUMMARIZING **B.** Read the information and look at the images of roses on this page and page 104. Add headings and make notes in the Venn diagram to create a summary.

Two of the most popular types of rose plants are the hybrid tea and the floribunda. As cut flowers, they sell in large numbers around the world, and the plants are also commonly grown in people's gardens. While similar in appearance, the two flowers have a number of differences. The hybrid tea has large, single flowers on each stem, whereas floribundas produce groups of smaller flowers on a single stem. The hybrid tea plant is also taller than the floribunda. Hybrid teas can grow to more than two meters in height, but the floribunda rarely grows higher than one meter.

^ The flowers of a floribunda rose plant

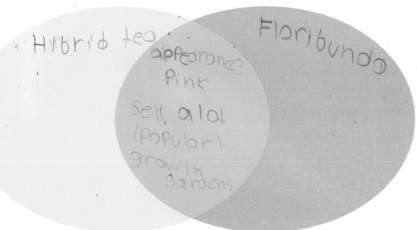

Hybrid tea
appearance
Pink
Sell alot
(popular)
grow in gardens
Floribunda

COMPLETION
A. Complete the information using the words in the box.

considerable	exported	handle	industry	prevents

In the flower ¹ _industry_, speed is important. Getting fresh roses from Colombia to the United States in just a few days requires ² _considerable_ effort. Pickers first cut the roses in the early morning because the cool morning air ³ _prevents_ the roses from drying out. The next morning, the roses are put into boxes and trucked to Bogotá Airport to be ⁴ _exported_ to the United States. The roses arrive at markets in various U.S. cities the following day. These markets ⁵ _handle_ the huge task of sorting them. Finally, the flowers are sent to florists to be sold.

WORDS IN CONTEXT
B. Complete the sentences. Choose the correct options.

1. A company that **dominates** other companies _____.
   a. (beats them in business)   b. assists them

2. If you **assume** something, you _____.
   a. (accept it is true without evidence)   b. have evidence to prove it is true

3. Something that is **claimed** to be true is _____ true.
   a. definitely   b. (said to be)

4. If an event is **predictable**, you are _____ it will happen.
   a. not sure   b. (sure)

5. When you **invest** in something, you _____.
   a. (put effort or money into it)   b. get money or things from it

WORD LINK
C. The words **predictable** and **preventable** are formed using the suffix *-able*. The suffix, often meaning "able to be," can be added to other words. Complete the sentences with the words in the box. Check your spelling in a dictionary.

enjoy	like	notice	value

1. Be careful with that vase. It's very _value_**able**.
2. We had a really _enjoy_**able** afternoon at the flower market.
3. He's a really _lik_**able** person. I get along very well with him.
4. There has been a _notic_**able** improvement in working conditions in the flower industry.

BEFORE YOU READ

DEFINITIONS **A.** Look at the photo and read the caption. Match each word in **bold** with its definition.

1. brand   a. companies in the same industry with similar customers

2. competitors   b. the name and image that identifies a certain product

3. marketing   c. the action of promoting or selling products

DISCUSSION **B.** What methods do perfume companies use to make people buy their products? Discuss with a partner and list some ideas. Then skim the passage to see which of your ideas are mentioned.

∧ In order to make their **brands** stand out from **competitors**, perfume companies spend millions of dollars on **marketing**.

THE POWER OF PERFUME

To make a good perfume, scientists work with scent experts to find and mix the right scents.

A "Perfume," says expert perfumer Sophia Grojsman, "is a promise in a bottle." That promise might be reflected in a perfume's name: *Joy* or *Pleasure,* for example. Millions of dollars are spent on the marketing of a perfume so that customers connect a fragrance to luxury, attraction, or a certain **attitude**.

B Fragrances can have power over our thoughts and emotions. Scientists believe memory and smell are closely connected in our brains, and that certain aromas have the power to call up deep memories. Perfume makers are especially aware of this and use scents that touch us deeply.

C In the perfume world, an *essence* is a material with its own special aroma. Some are natural, and often **derived** from flowers and plants. Others are synthetic[1] copies of rare or difficult-to-**obtain** essences. Perfume **authority** Harry Frémont says a good fragrance "is a balance between naturals and synthetics. Naturals give richness and roundness; synthetics, backbone and sparkle."

D Hundreds of new perfumes are put on the market every year. Of these, few become successful. It's a risky business. A company introducing a new scent can easily run through a **budget** of 20 million dollars. **Profits**, however, can be very high. One successful fragrance, *CK One* from designer Calvin Klein, made 250 million dollars in its first year.

Image and Marketing

E In a Paris perfume store—a building of shining stone, metal, and glass—famous perfumes are displayed and **guarded** like the works of art in the nearby Louvre Museum.[2] Salespeople are dressed smartly in black, and each type of perfume is sold in a **distinctively** shaped bottle. In perfume sales, the **emphasis** is on presentation at least as much as on the product.

Former baseball player Derek Jeter advertises his scent, a cologne named *Driven.*

F So, naturally, France's main competitor in the global perfume market is the United States, where image is all-important. **Celebrity**-branded scents fill the market, each preceded by advertisements and TV appearances designed to create hype.[3] Even sports celebrities— like baseball star Derek Jeter—are creating their own fragrance brands.

G It is easy to be confused about which perfume to buy. Perfumer Annie Buzantian offers this advice: You really can't get an idea whether a perfume works or not until you wear it. "It's like the difference between a dress on the hanger and a dress on your body," says Buzantian. Though Frémont adds, "Your first impression is often the right one."

---

1 If a material is **synthetic**, it is made by humans.
2 The **Louvre Museum** is a world-famous art museum in Paris, France.
3 If something creates **hype**, it raises a lot of interest and excitement.

A. Choose the best answer for each question.

MAIN IDEA

1. What is the main idea of the first paragraph?

a. Perfume companies spend a lot of money developing their brand.
b. Bottle design is one of the most important features of a perfume.
c. Perfumes provide a lot of joy and pleasure to customers.

DETAIL

2. According to Harry Frémont, a good fragrance is a balance between _____.

a. flower and wood essences
b. rare and very common essences
c. natural and man-made essences

VOCABULARY

3. In paragraph D, the phrase *run through* is closest in meaning to _____.

a. use up
b. produce
c. earn

INFERENCE

4. What is probably the main reason the perfumes in the Paris store are so well guarded?

a. The store has been robbed many times.
b. It is a way to impress customers.
c. French stores are normally well guarded.

DETAIL

5. What does Annie Buzantian suggest people do when buying a perfume?

a. Try it before you buy it.
b. Buy different perfumes for different days.
c. Buy the best perfume that you can afford.

Civet—an essence derived from material taken from the talls of civets—is a valued ingredient in perfumes.

SUMMARIZING

B. Complete the summary using words from the reading.

Perfume companies spend a lot of time and money on creating and marketing their products. Fragrances can influence our thoughts and ¹ Emotions , and have the power to call up our distant ² memories Perfume makers know this and use aromas that are able to touch us deeply. Presentation is also very important. Salespeople dress very ³ smartly , and many perfumes are sold in uniquely shaped ⁴ bottles . Companies also use well-known ⁵ celebrities to help advertise their fragrance.

Recognizing and Understanding Synonyms

A synonym is a word that has the same meaning as another word. Writers often use them to avoid repeating the same words and to add variety to their writing. Knowledge of synonyms can greatly help your reading comprehension.

It is often possible to guess the meaning of unknown synonyms from the context in which they are used. For example, in the sentences below, we can guess that the word *huge* is a synonym of *large*.

> *Large* amounts of money are spent on marketing perfumes. However, *huge* spending does not always result in high profits.

When you learn new vocabulary, it is a good idea to also list any synonyms. You can check for synonyms in a dictionary or thesaurus. If a synonym has a slightly different meaning, note the difference: *perfume (for women) = cologne (for men)*.

RECOGNIZING SYNONYMS

A. Look back at paragraph B from the reading passage. Find and underline two synonyms for the noun *smell*.

UNDERSTANDING SYNONYMS

B. The words below are also synonyms for the noun *smell*. Check them in a dictionary or thesaurus. Do the words generally have a positive or a negative meaning?

odor	stench	stink

RECOGNIZING SYNONYMS

C. In each set of sentences, find and underline a synonym for the word in **bold**.

1. A store needs to consider how to **present** any new fragrance. For example, it may choose to display it at its own counter with several salespeople offering samples.

2. There are many **successful** men's colognes on the market today. One of the most popular is *Bleu de Chanel*.

3. Smart shoppers should check the **price** before they decide to purchase a perfume as the cost of some perfumes can be over 100 dollars.

CRITICAL THINKING Applying Ideas   Work with a partner and brainstorm ideas for a new perfume or cologne. First choose a target customer (e.g., males between the ages of 20 and 30) and then think of ways to market the product. Share your ideas with the class.

Target customer: _____ Male people _____

Name of perfume or cologne: _____ Maritine time _____

Bottle shape / color: _____ Blue with shape of whale _____

Celebrity to feature in ads: _____ Chris evans _____

Other marketing ideas: _____ An slogan that says feel the smell of the 2 seas. _____

COMPLETION   **A.** Complete the information using the words in the box.

budget   derived   distinctive   obtain   profits

For many years, a material known as *ambergris* was used in perfumes. Ambergris comes from certain sperm whales. Perfume companies often [1] _obtain_ it from collectors who find it floating on the ocean or lying on a beach. Ambergris has a very [2] _distinctive_ aroma. Because it's not easy to get, it's expensive and can often be beyond the [3] _budget_ of many perfume makers. To maintain [4] _profits_, more synthetic scents—partly [5] _derived_ from plants— are used to create similar aromas.

Ambergris can cost up to $20 per gram. Buying and selling it is illegal in many countries.

WORDS IN
CONTEXT
B. Complete the sentences. Choose the correct options.

1. If you are asked to **guard** some jewelry, you make sure _b_.
   a. nobody steals it   b. you get a good price for it

2. An **authority** on perfume _a_.
   a. owns a lot of it   b. knows a lot about it

3. A **celebrity** is someone who _b_.
   a. makes perfume   b. is famous

4. If you put **emphasis** on a word when you speak, the word is probably _a_.
   a. important   b. not important

5. Your **attitude** toward something is _b_ about it.
   a. how you feel   b. what you know

COLLOCATIONS   **C.** The nouns in the box are often used with the word **distinctive**. Complete the sentences with the correct words. One word is extra.

feature   pattern   smell   sound

1. This gas has a distinctive _smell_, but it's not dangerous.
2. The distinctive _pattern_ of zebra stripes helps them hide from predators.
3. A distinctive _feature_ of the hybrid tea rose is its long stem.

A worker prepares fair trade roses at Nevado Rose Farm in Latacúnga, Ecuador.

FLOWERS FROM ECUADOR

BEFORE YOU WATCH

PREVIEWING **A.** Read the information. The words and phrases in **bold** appear in the video. Match each word with its definition.

In some places where flowers are grown, workers receive very low **wages** and work long hours in poor conditions. In recent years, however, more and more companies in the flower industry have started to **operate** under *fair trade* rules. These rules ensure that workers have acceptable working conditions and fair pay. Ecuador is just one country where large numbers of workers have benefited from improved **employment** practices.

1. employment •   • a. (n) working for money

2. operate •   • b. (n) the money paid to a worker

3. wages •   • c. (v) to do business

DISCUSSION **B.** What do you remember about Ecuador's flower industry from Reading A? Discuss the questions with a partner. Look back at Reading A to check your answers.

1. Why is Ecuador a good place to grow flowers?

2. How are Ecuadorian roses different from other roses?

GIST **A.** Watch the video. Match each person with the correct description.

1. Robin Peñaherrera •   • a. works for the Ecuador government.
2. Allan Woods •   • b. is very busy on Valentine's Day.
3. Nathalie Cely •   • c. owns a company that exports flowers.

COMPLETION **B.** Watch the video again. Complete the summary with the numbers in the box. Two numbers are extra.

25	50	100	660	4,000	60,000

In a single year, Ecuador may export around [1]$ _660_ million in roses to the United States, and around [2] _22 2_ percent of roses in the United States come from Ecuador. The flower trade has given a huge boost to Ecuador's economy. The industry has created around [3] _60,000_ jobs in the country, around [4] _50_ percent of which have been filled by women.

CRITICAL THINKING Evaluating Pros and Cons   Imagine you are ordering roses online. What are the pros and cons of buying from each company below? Which roses would you buy? Discuss with a partner.

Company Description	Price of 10 roses	Flower quality	Follows fair trade rules?
A small company in your local area	$30	High	No
A medium-size company based overseas	$25	High	Yes
A large international company based overseas	$29	Average	No

VOCABULARY REVIEW

Do you remember the meanings of these words? Check (✓) the ones you know. Look back at the unit and review any words you're not sure of.

Reading A

☐ assume   ☐ claim   ☐ considerable*   ☐ dominate*   ☐ export*

☐ handle   ☐ industry   ☐ invest*   ☐ predictable*   ☐ prevent

Reading B

☐ attitude*   ☐ authority*   ☐ budget   ☐ celebrity   ☐ derive*

☐ distinctively*   ☐ emphasis*   ☐ guard   ☐ obtain*   ☐ profits

* Academic Word List

8

GREAT EXPLORERS

Many early explorers traveled the world by ship, spending months and even years at sea.

Discuss these questions with a partner.

1. Who are some great explorers from history? What are they well known for?

2. What do present-day explorers do?

BEFORE YOU READ

READING MAPS **A.** Look at the map of the explorer Marco Polo's journey with his father and uncle. Then answer the questions.

    1. When and where did the Polos start and finish their trip? For how many years did they travel?

    2. What were some of the farthest places they reached during their travels?

    3. What other places did they visit? What do you know about these places?

PREDICTING **B.** Why do you think the Polos went on such a long journey? Discuss with a partner. Read the passage to check your ideas.

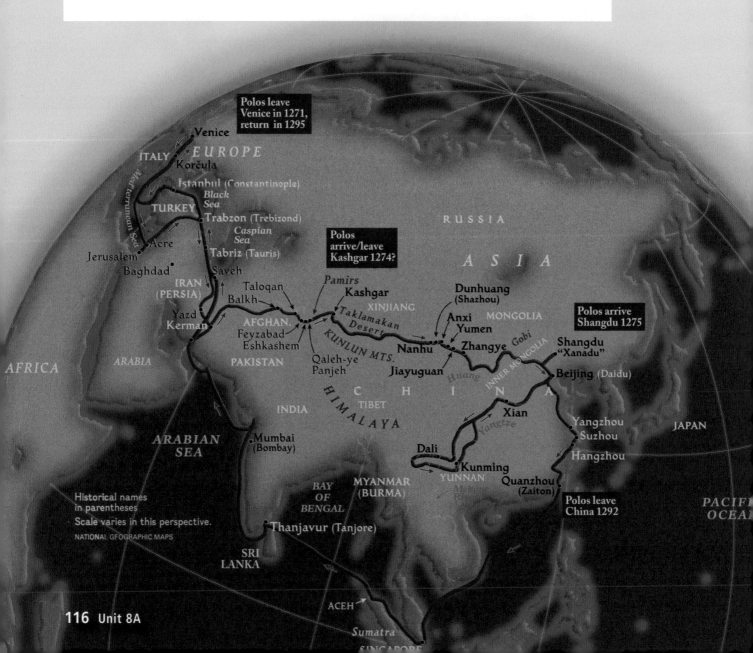

AN INCREDIBLE
JOURNEY

A The Polos—Marco, his father, Niccolò, and his uncle, Maffeo—had been traveling for three and a half years when they finally achieved their **objective**—a long-awaited meeting with the powerful Mongol leader Kublai Khan. The historic event took place in 1275 at the Khan's luxurious summer capital[1] in Shangdu, in what is now northern China. Kublai Khan was surprisingly **informal** as he greeted his tired guests: "Welcome, gentlemen! Please stand up. How've you been? How was the trip?"

B Marco Polo's trip had, in fact, started more than 9,000 kilometers away in Venice when he was just a teenager. His father and uncle already knew Kublai Khan from a previous visit nine years earlier, when they had spent a short time in Shangdu. On this second trip, the Polos stayed for 17 years before they returned home. They made themselves useful to the Khan, and **undertook** various missions[2] and tasks for him. It is likely that the Khan **considered** it an honor[3] that these Europeans—who were rare in China—had made this extremely difficult journey, and he took the opportunity to make good use of their skills and knowledge.

C While he was in the service of Kublai Khan, "the most powerful man in people and in lands and in treasure that ever was in the world," Marco Polo was able to learn and experience many things that were new to Europeans. In his travel **journal**, he wrote that Kublai Khan's palace was the greatest he had ever seen. He **admired** the Khan's recently completed new capital—Daidu—whose streets were "so straight and so broad." The city was located in what is now the center of Beijing, and Kublai Khan's city planning can still be **perceived** in the straight, broad streets of China's modern capital.

---

1 The **capital** of a country is the city where its government meets.
2 A **mission** is an important task, especially one that involves traveling.
3 Something that is an **honor** is special and desirable.

> A statue of Marco Polo in Zhenglan Banner, China, close to where Polo is thought to have met Mongol leader Kublai Khan

D We learn from Marco Polo that, in the administration of his empire, Kublai Khan made use of a fast and simple message system. Horse riders spaced every 40 kilometers allowed messages to cover 500 kilometers a day. As soon as one horse had run 40 kilometers, the next horse would run the next 40 kilometers, and so on. Marco also learned the secret of asbestos cloth, which is made from a mineral[4] and doesn't catch fire. Paper money also took him by surprise, since it was not yet used in the West at that time. Homes were heated with "black stones … which burn like logs." Those stones were coal—unknown in most of Europe—and were so plentiful that many people had a hot bath three times a week.

E Although the Khan did not want his visitors to leave, the Polos finally received **permission** to return home in 1292. Marco continued his **observations** while on the ocean **voyage** by way of Sumatra and India. After he returned home, Marco completed a book about his trip, full of details about his amazing cultural experiences. It was probably the single greatest contribution to geographical knowledge ever made to the West about the East.

4 A **mineral** is a substance that is found naturally in rocks and in the earth.

> An ancient fort in Jiayuguan, China—a location
> Marco Polo is likely to have traveled through

READING COMPREHENSION

A. Choose the best answer for each question.

GIST   **1.** What is the reading mainly about?

   a. Marco Polo's relationship with his father
   b. why Marco Polo's travels are important
   c. how Marco Polo was able to reach China

DETAIL   **2.** What was surprising about the Polos' meeting with the Khan?

   a. He lived in a luxurious palace.
   b. He spoke to them in a casual way.
   c. He didn't remember them from a previous visit.

DETAIL   **3.** Kublai Khan used _____ to deliver messages to his people.

   a. runners
   b. the Polos
   c. horse riders

INFERENCE   **4.** Marco Polo saw that asbestos cloth, paper money, and coal were used in the East. According to the passage, this shows that _____.

   a. the West already knew about and used these inventions
   b. the West had forgotten the technologies used in the East
   c. the East was ahead of the West in some areas of technology

REFERENCE   **5.** In the last sentence of paragraph E, the word *It* refers to _____.

   a. a book
   b. culture
   c. Marco Polo's journey

SEQUENCING   **B.** Add the events (a–f) to the timeline.

   a. Marco Polo writes a book.

   b. Niccolò, Maffeo, and Marco Polo leave China.
   c. Niccolò, Maffeo, and Marco Polo visit India and Sumatra.
   d. Niccolò, Maffeo, and Marco Polo meet Kublai Khan.
   e. Niccolò, Maffeo, and Marco Polo start their journey and leave Venice.
   f. Niccolò and Maffeo Polo meet Kublai Khan.

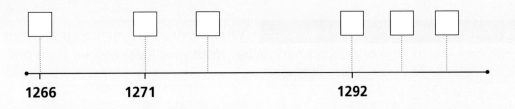

1266   1271   1292

Taking Notes on a Reading (1)

Note-taking can help you stay focused while reading and will allow you to better understand and analyze a text. Here are some tips:

1. Summarize in your own words. Doing so will help you engage more with the passage. If you want to quote directly from the text, use quotation marks (" ").

2. Use headings, bullet points, and numbering systems to organize information and present it clearly.

3. Keep your notes short. Write down only the key words and ideas. Consider using abbreviations to save time. For example:

• Use standard abbreviations	w/ = with b/c = because e.g. = for example
• Use initials	USA = United States EU = European Union
• Write 1–2 syllables	esp = especially approx = approximately
• Write only consonants	hr = hour wk = week yr = year

TAKING NOTES   **A.** Complete the notes below using a word or number from the reading passage.

MP's journey to China
- Started in Venice when MP was a ¹_____
- Approx ²_____ km
- Stayed in Shangdu for ³_____ yrs, left 1292
- Helped ⁴_____ w/ various tasks
- KK "considered it an honor" b/c ⁵_____ rare in China

MP's observations
- KK had amazing palace
- Impressed by capital, Daidu (now center of ⁶_____)
- KK had fast ⁷_____ system w/ horse riders
- Learned about: 1. asbestos cloth, 2. ⁸_____ money, 3. coal

Why important?
- Used notes to complete a ⁹_____
- Considered "single greatest contribution to geographical knowledge" about East to the West

CRITICAL THINKING Inferring Information   Who do you think gained more from the Polos' visit to China—Marco Polo or Kublai Khan? Why? Note your ideas below. Then discuss with a partner.

_____

_____

_____

VOCABULARY PRACTICE

DEFINITIONS **A.** Complete the definitions using the words in the box.

| informal   objective   observations   perceive   permission |

1. Your _____ is what you are trying to achieve.
2. To _____ something means to see it.
3. Your _____ are what you see or notice.
4. If you have _____ to do something, you are allowed to do it.
5. If a situation is _____, it is usually relaxed, friendly, or unofficial.

COMPLETION **B.** Complete the information. Circle the correct words.

After surviving the dangers of the ocean [1]**voyage / observation**
from China, Marco Polo reached his home city of Venice. But more
troubles awaited him there. At that time, cities in Italy were
often at war with each other. During fighting between Venice
and a neighboring city, Marco Polo was put in prison. There,
he met Rustichello, a writer of fairy tales. Polo wanted to create
a(n) [2]**journal / objective** of his travels, and he asked the

Marco Polo

writer for his help. Rustichello agreed to [3]**undertake / observe** the task. Because of
this book, many people began to [4]**undertake / admire** Polo's achievements. Today,
Marco Polo is [5]**admired / considered** by many to be one of the greatest explorers
that ever lived.

WORD FORMS **C.** The verbs **observe** and **admire** follow similar patterns when changing to other
parts of speech. Complete the sentences using the correct form of the words in
the box.

verb	noun	noun (person)	adjective
observe	observation	observer	observable
admire	admiration	admirer	admirable

1. He has many _____ qualities, but patience isn't one of them.
2. With modern telescopes, scientists are able to _____ the most
   distant galaxies.
3. Marco Polo recorded his _____ in a travel journal.
4. We know that Marco Polo was a great _____ of Kublai Khan's palace.

BEFORE YOU READ

READING MAPS **A.** Look at the map and read the caption. Try to guess the answers to these questions.

    1. Who traveled farther, Ibn Battuta or Marco Polo?

    2. How many places did Ibn Battuta visit?

    3. For how many years was Ibn Battuta traveling?

SCANNING **B.** Now quickly read the first two paragraphs of the reading passage to check your guesses.

Ibn Battuta was born in Tangier, in what is now Morocco. He traveled to many places around the world in the 14th century.

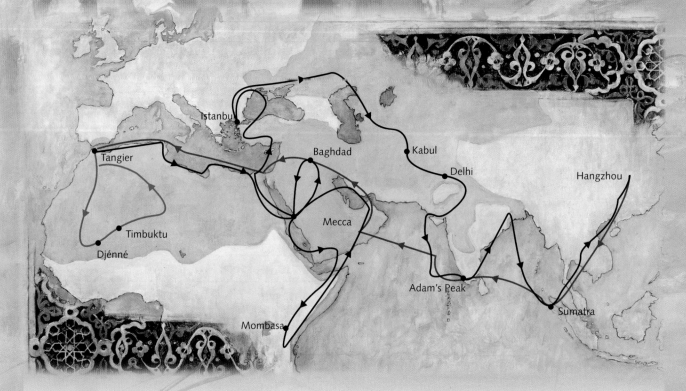

The travels of Ibn Battuta

| | Islamic lands, 14th century | ▶ Route from Tangier to China | ▶ Return route | ▶ Round trip in Sahara |

THE TRAVELS OF IBN BATTUTA

A "I left Tangier, my birthplace, the 13th of June, 1325, with the **intention** of making the pilgrimage[1] [to Mecca] … to leave all my friends both female and male, to **abandon** my home as birds abandon their nests." So begins an old manuscript[2] in a library in Paris—the travel journal of Ibn Battuta.

B Almost two centuries before Columbus, this young Moroccan set off for Mecca, returning home three decades later. Ibn Battuta is now **regarded** as one of history's great travelers. Driven by curiosity, he journeyed to remote corners of the Islamic world, traveling three times as far as Marco Polo, through 44 modern countries. He is little celebrated in some parts of the world, yet his name is well known among Arabs. In his hometown of Tangier, a square, a hotel, a café, a ferry boat, and even a hamburger are named after him.

C **Prior** to his adventures traveling the world, Ibn Battuta studied in Mecca for several years. However, the urge to travel soon took over. He traveled to India, seeking profitable employment with the Sultan[3] of Delhi. On the way, he described his group being attacked in the open country by 80 foot soldiers and two horsemen: "we fought … killing one of their horsemen and about twelve of the foot soldiers. … I was hit by an arrow and my horse by another, but God in his grace preserved me."

D In Delhi, the sultan gave him the position of judge, based on his studies at Mecca. But the sultan had an unpredictable character, and Ibn Battuta was soon looking for an opportunity to leave. When the sultan offered to **finance** a trip to China, Ibn Battuta agreed. He set off in three ships, but **misfortune** struck while he was still on shore. A sudden storm grounded and broke up two of the ships. Scattering[4] treasure, the storm drowned many people and horses. As he watched, the third ship, with all his **belongings** and slaves, was carried out to sea and never heard from again.

E After a lifetime of adventures, Ibn Battuta was finally ordered by the Sultan of Morocco to return home to share his **wisdom** with the world. Fortunately, he **consented** and wrote a book that has been **translated** into numerous languages, allowing people everywhere to read about his incredible journeys.

---

1 A **pilgrimage** is a trip to a place of religious importance.

2 A **manuscript** is a piece of writing that is handwritten, or an early version of a book.

3 A **sultan** is a ruler in some Islamic countries.

4 If things are **scattered**, they have been thrown or dropped so they are spread all over an area.

A. Choose the best answer for each question.

GIST **1.** What is the best description of Ibn Battuta?

    a. an amazing writer from Europe
    b. one of history's great adventurers
    c. the first man to sail around the world

DETAIL **2.** The Sultan of Delhi gave Ibn Battuta the position of judge because _____.

    a. Ibn Battuta had studied in Mecca
    b. Ibn Battuta had been a judge before
    c. Ibn Battuta had traveled to many countries

REFERENCE **3.** What does the word *he* refer to in the last sentence of paragraph E?

    a. Ibn Battuta
    b. the Sultan of Morocco
    c. Ibn Battuta's slave

DETAIL **4.** Why did Ibn Battuta finally return home?

    a. He was tired of traveling.
    b. He feared the Sultan of Delhi.
    c. The Sultan of Morocco told him to return.

The Ibn Battuta shopping mall in Dubai has six sections named after areas of the world he visited.

INFERENCE **5.** The writer of this passage most likely thinks that Ibn Battuta's journey _____.

    a. was inspired by Marco Polo's travels
    b. was common for people of that time
    c. should be more well known today

SCANNING **B.** Write short answers to the questions below. Use two or three words from the passage for each answer.

1. Where is Ibn Battuta's travel journal now?

_____

2. What three places in Tangier are named after Ibn Battuta?

_____

3. How long did Battuta study in Mecca?

_____

4. What destroyed the ships Battuta was planning to take to China?

_____

Taking Notes on a Reading (2)—Using a Concept Map

An alternative way of taking notes on a reading is by using a concept map. A concept map can help organize information in a more memorable way.

If the reading is about a specific person or thing, a common way to organize a concept map is to start with a circle containing the person or thing's name. Around the circle, note the main ideas that the reading covers, and, finally, the key details. Draw lines to connect the ideas.

TAKING NOTES **A. Complete the concept map using information from the reading.**

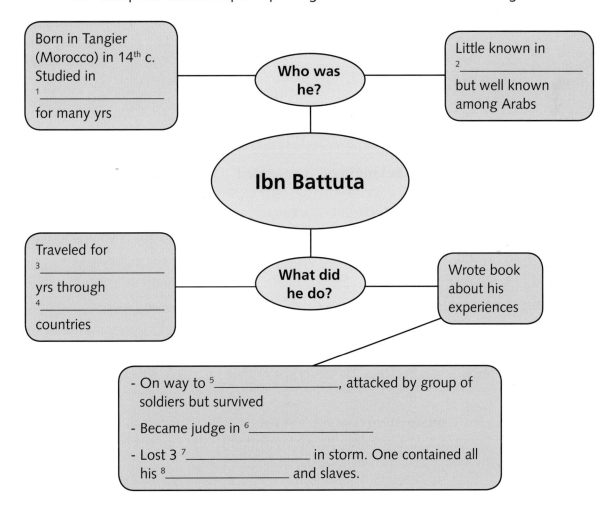

Born in Tangier (Morocco) in 14th c. Studied in 1_____ for many yrs

Who was he?

Little known in 2_____ but well known among Arabs

Ibn Battuta

Traveled for 3_____ yrs through 4_____ countries

What did he do?

Wrote book about his experiences

- On way to 5_____, attacked by group of soldiers but survived
- Became judge in 6_____
- Lost 3 7_____ in storm. One contained all his 8_____ and slaves.

CRITICAL THINKING Applying Ideas

▶ Think of a famous historical figure from your country. Make notes about their life using a concept map similar to the one above.

▶ Use your notes to describe the person to your partner.

DEFINITIONS **A.** Read the information below. Then complete the definitions using the words in **red**.

During his travels, Ibn Battuta suffered many **misfortunes**. In his final journey, he traveled to Mali, with the **intention** of meeting a king who was **regarded** as extremely generous. He was even said to give his guests gifts of gold. However, **prior** to Ibn Battuta's arrival, the old king died. The new king, Mansa Sulayman, only gave Ibn Battuta a little food. When he saw his gift, Ibn Battuta could only laugh.

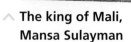

1. If you are _____ as having a certain quality, people believe you have that quality.

2. If you have the _____ of doing something, you have decided to do it.

3. A person's _____ are bad or unlucky things that happen to them.

4. If something happens _____ to something else, it happens first.

⌃ **The king of Mali, Mansa Sulayman**

COMPLETION **B.** Complete the sentences below with the words in the box.

abandoned	belongings	consented	financed	translated	wisdom

1. The writings of Ibn Battuta have been _____ into all major languages.

2. The king and queen of Spain _____ Columbus's voyage to the New World.

3. Kublai Khan finally _____ to the Polos' request to return to Europe.

4. A good king is one who has great _____ and makes good decisions.

5. To get deeper into the forest, the explorers _____ their vehicle and continued on foot.

6. Nobody was hurt, but the family lost all their _____ in the fire.

WORD PARTS **C.** The word **misfortune** contains the prefix *mis-*, which usually means "badly" or "incorrectly." Complete the sentences with the correct form of the words in the box.

behaved	heard	placed	spelled

1. You mis_____ this word in your essay. It's *prior*, not *prier*.

2. Where is my passport? I think I mis_____ it.

3. The children mis_____ in class, so the teacher sent them out.

4. I thought he said the party started at 7, but I may have mis_____ him.

THE LEGEND OF MARCO POLO

∧ Marco Polo's travels included a long and difficult journey across the Taklamakan Desert.

BEFORE YOU WATCH

PREVIEWING **A.** Read the extracts from the video. Match each word in **bold** with its definition.

"The temperature of the desert is **formidable** in the summer."

"The hall is so vast that it could sit 6,000 for one **banquet**."

"The city was **excavated** in the 1930s …"

"Throughout the **province** of Cathay, there are large black stones dug from the mountains."

1. formidable •　　• a. an area within a country

2. banquet •　　• b. to remove earth carefully to find buried objects

3. excavate •　　• c. a large meal, usually for many people

4. province •　　• d. inspiring fear or respect by being large or powerful

PREDICTING **B.** Some historians do not believe that Marco Polo actually visited China. What could be some possible reasons? Note your ideas below. Then discuss with a partner.

_____

_____

_____

GIST **A.** Watch the video. Check the questions that are answered.

a. ☐ Why was Polo put in jail?

b. ☐ Who helped Polo write his travel book?

c. ☐ When did Polo begin his journey to China?

d. ☐ What was Polo's desert journey probably like?

e. ☐ How did Polo describe the Khan's summer palace?

f. ☐ How many languages has Polo's book been translated into?

DETAIL **B.** Watch the video again. Do the following descriptions give support **for** or **against** the claim that Polo visited China? Write **F** (for) or **A** (against) for each.

Polo's description of ...

a. a battle that took place in China   _____

b. a large and unusual animal   _____

c. a material that can be used as fuel   _____

d. an extremely large hall   _____

CRITICAL THINKING Evaluating Arguments

▶ Which argument do you think is stronger—that Marco Polo did or didn't visit China? Why? Discuss with a partner.

▶ Look back at Reading A. Does the reading give a balanced argument, or does it support only one side of the argument?

VOCABULARY REVIEW

Do you remember the meanings of these words? Check (✓) the ones you know. Look back at the unit and review any words you're not sure of.

Reading A

☐ admire	☐ consider	☐ informal	☐ journal*	☐ objective*
☐ observation	☐ perceive*	☐ permission	☐ undertake*	☐ voyage

Reading B

☐ abandon*	☐ belongings	☐ consent*	☐ finance*	☐ intention
☐ misfortune	☐ prior*	☐ regard	☐ translate	☐ wisdom

* Academic Word List

9

IDENTITY

WARM UP

Discuss these questions with a partner.

1. In what ways do you look similar to your parents?

2. How are you different now from when you were younger?

Fraternal twins like Marcia (left) and Millie Biggs often look quite different from each other.

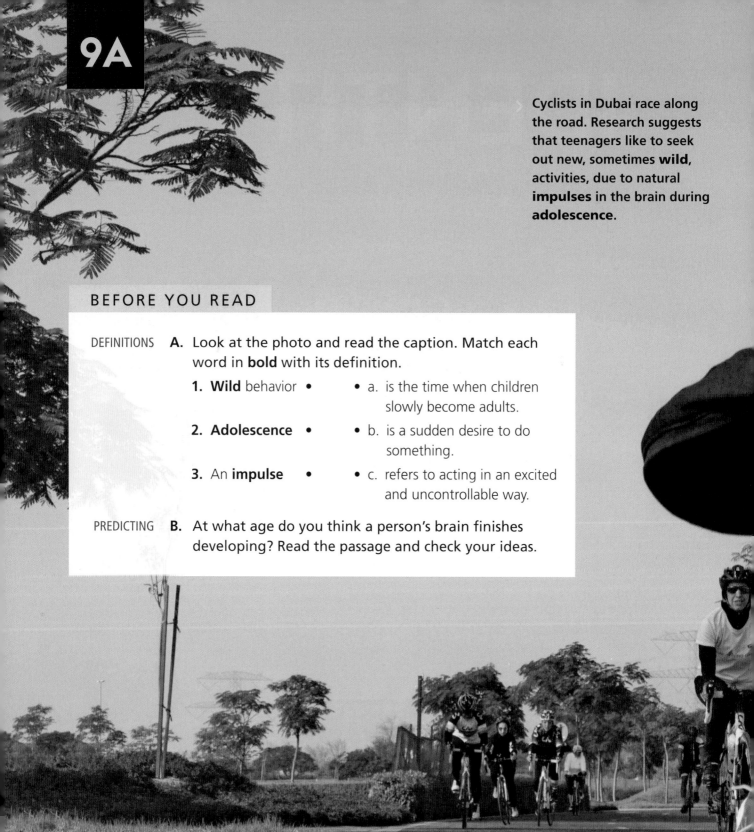

Cyclists in Dubai race along the road. Research suggests that teenagers like to seek out new, sometimes **wild**, activities, due to natural **impulses** in the brain during **adolescence**.

BEFORE YOU READ

DEFINITIONS **A.** Look at the photo and read the caption. Match each word in **bold** with its definition.

1. **Wild** behavior •
      • a. is the time when children slowly become adults.

2. **Adolescence** •
      • b. is a sudden desire to do something.

3. An **impulse** •
      • c. refers to acting in an excited and uncontrollable way.

PREDICTING **B.** At what age do you think a person's brain finishes developing? Read the passage and check your ideas.

THE TEENAGE BRAIN

A Parents, teachers, and anyone who regularly **deals with** teenagers knows how difficult the adolescent years can be. Adolescents have always been known to do wild—even dangerous—things. This was thought to be due to the foolishness[1] of youth. Now, brain-imaging technology allows scientists to study the physical development of the brain in more detail than ever before. Their discoveries have led to a new theory of why teens act the way they do.

A Work in Progress

B Recently, scientists discovered that though our brains are almost at their full size by the age of six, they are far from fully developed. Only during adolescence do our brains truly "grow up." During this time, they **go through** great changes, like a computer system being **upgraded**. This "upgrade" was once thought to be finished by about age 12. Now, scientists have **concluded** that our brains continue to change until age 25. Such changes make us better at balancing our impulses with the need to follow rules. However, a still-developing brain does this clumsily.[2] The result, scientists claim, is the unpredictable behavior seen in teenagers.

---

1 **Foolishness** refers to the behavior of someone who makes bad decisions.
2 If something is done **clumsily**, it is done in an awkward or uncontrolled way.

Pleasure Seekers

C The studies confirm that teens are more likely to take **risks** and behave in extreme ways. Fortunately, the news isn't all negative. As brain scientist B. J. Casey points out, the teen brain inspires such behavior in order to help teenagers prepare for adult life.

D One way the brain does this is by changing the way teens measure risk and **reward**. Researchers found that when teens think about rewards, their brains release more of the chemicals that create **pleasure** than an adult brain would. Researchers believe this makes the rewards seem more important than the risks, and makes teens feel the **excitement** of new experiences more keenly than adults do.

E Research into the structure of the teen brain also found that it makes social connections seem especially rewarding. As such, teens have an **intense** need to meet new people. Scientists suggest this is because as teens, we begin to **realize** that our peers may one day control the world we live in. Because it is still developing, a teen brain can change to deal with new situations. It therefore connects social rewards with even more pleasure. In this way, the brain encourages teens to have a wide circle of friends, which is believed to make us more successful in life.

F Unfortunately, this hunt for greater rewards can sometimes lead teens to make bad decisions. However, it also means that teens are more likely, and less afraid, to try new things or to be independent. The scientists' findings suggest that in the long run, the impulses of the teen brain are what help teens leave their parents' care and live their own lives successfully.

❮ Two teenagers hang out in a diner.

A. Choose the best answer for each question.

PURPOSE

1. What is the main purpose of the reading?

    a. to suggest that today's teenagers think differently from previous generations

    b. to explain how teenagers' brains affect their behavior

    c. to describe an experiment that looked at the brains of teenagers

DETAIL

2. Which of the following statements about an adolescent's brain is NOT true?

    a. It can change to deal with new situations.

    b. It is better than an adult brain at following rules.

    c. It is still developing.

PARAPHRASING

3. In paragraph C, what does the author mean by *the news isn't all negative*?

    a. The negative side of the research is not understood.

    b. The way the teen brain works has some advantages.

    c. The impulses of a teenage brain should be controlled.

VOCABULARY

4. In paragraph D, what does *keenly* mean?

    a. strongly

    b. loudly

    c. slowly

MAIN IDEA

5. Which of the following would be the best heading for the last paragraph?

    a. An Independent Brain

    b. The Rewards of Friendship

    c. The Parents' Role

SUMMARIZING

B. Complete the sentences. Use one to three words from the passage for each answer.

1. Scientists are now better able to study the physical development of the brain thanks to improvements in _____ technology.

2. By the age of _____, a child's brain is almost at its full size.

3. Teenagers' brains go through an upgrade similar to that of a(n) _____.

4. Scientists now know that our brains continue to change until the age of _____.

5. Teenagers' brains measure risk and reward differently than _____ brains do.

6. Some believe that having a _____ of friends makes us more successful in life.

7. Teens are not afraid to try new things. This makes it easier for them when they eventually leave their _____.

Understanding Claims

Many articles and scientific texts cite research or expert opinions to support claims put forth by the writer. One way to understand the strength of a claim is to look closely at the verbs used. Verbs such as *find (out), point out, know, discover,* and *conclude* show a high degree of confidence in the claims being presented. Verbs such as *suggest, think, believe,* and *claim* show a lower degree of confidence.

SCANNING   **A. Look back at Reading A. Find and underline the claims below.**

1. A person's brain reaches almost its full size by the age of six.

2. The brain goes through a process of great change, which actually continues until age 25.

3. The result of a still-developing and clumsy brain is the unpredictable behavior seen in teenagers.

4. Teens are more likely to take risks and behave in extreme ways.

5. The teen brain makes rewards seem more important than risks, and teens feel new experiences more keenly.

6. In the long run, the impulses of the teen brain help teens live their own lives successfully.

∧ **A teenage girl in Tokyo's Harajuku area**

UNDERSTANDING CLAIMS   **B. Identify and write the verbs in the passage that are used to make the claims in activity A. Then mark each claim as showing a high (H) degree or a lower (L) degree of confidence.**

1. *discovered* _____   H   L   4. _____   H   L

2. _____   H   L   5. _____   H   L

3. _____   H   L   6. _____   H   L

CRITICAL THINKING Reflecting   The reading passage states that we take the greatest risks when we are teenagers. At what age do you think people take the fewest risks? What things might affect a person's willingness to take risks? Note your ideas and then discuss with a partner.

_____

_____

_____

VOCABULARY PRACTICE

COMPLETION **A.** **Complete the information. Circle the correct words.**

Psychologist Laurence Steinberg has found that the biggest [1]**reward / risk** takers are 14- to 17-year-olds. This is not because they don't [2]**realize / go through** certain activities are dangerous, but because they value the [3]**rewards / upgrades** more than the risks. To test this idea, Steinberg uses a video game that involves driving a car. Players have to [4]**conclude / deal with** traffic lights that change quickly from green to red, forcing quick decisions. The study showed that when a friend was watching, teens took twice as many risks as when they played alone. From this, Steinberg [5]**went through / concluded** that social rewards can lead teens to take more risks.

WORDS IN
CONTEXT

B. **Complete the sentences. Choose the correct options.**

1. Something that would probably cause great **excitement** is _____.
   a. falling asleep while reading
   b. winning a sports event

2. If you **go through** a difficult time, you _____ it.
   a. avoid
   b. experience

3. Something that gives many people **pleasure** is _____.
   a. listening to music
   b. taking exams

4. When a machine gets **upgraded**, it should work _____.
   a. better
   b. worse

5. If a feeling is **intense**, it is very _____.
   a. strong
   b. weak

WORD WEB **C.** **Go through** is one of many phrasal verbs formed using the verb *go*. Complete the word web using the words in the box. Use a dictionary to help you.

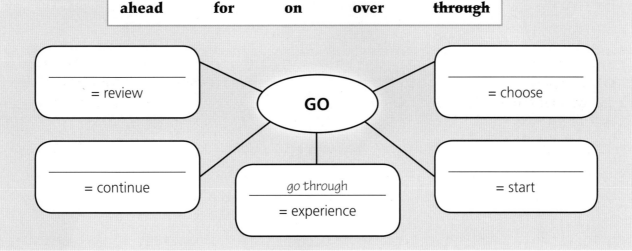

| ahead | for | on | over | ~~through~~ |

_____ = review

_____ = choose

GO

_____ = continue

go through _____ = experience

_____ = start

DEFINITIONS **A.** Look at the picture and read the caption. Then complete the sentences using the words in **bold**.

1. If two people have something _____, they are the same in some way.

2. A person's _____ is a number that represents their intelligence, based on their score on a special test.

3. If two things are exactly the same, we say they are _____.

4. The growth of our bodies follows a plan contained in our _____.

PREDICTING **B.** You are going to read about the Jim twins—identical twin brothers who were separated as babies but met when they were adults. In what ways do you think they were similar or different when they met? Discuss with a partner. Read the passage to check your ideas.

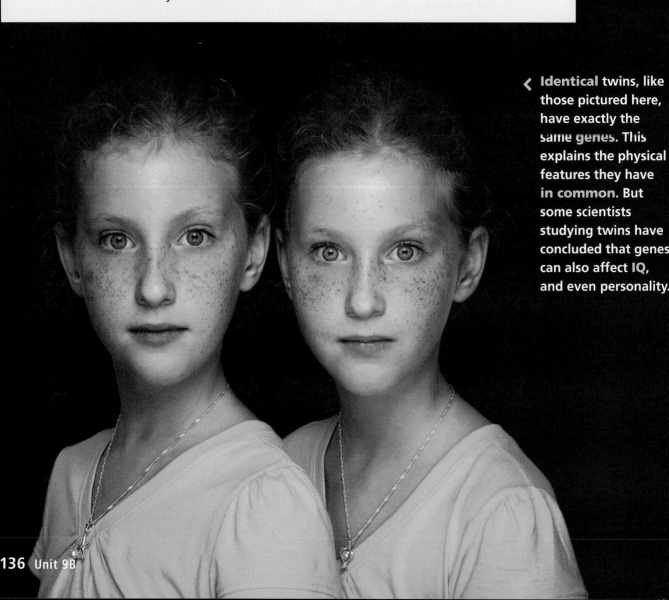

‹ **Identical** twins, like those pictured here, have exactly the **same genes**. This explains the physical features they have **in common**. But some scientists studying twins have concluded that genes can also affect **IQ**, and even personality.

SEEING
DOUBLE

A Many scientists once believed that physical similarities between identical twins are **genetic**, while their personalities, intelligence, and other differences between them are an effect of their environment. But scientists are now discovering that the **boundaries** between genetics and environment are not so clear after all.

The Jim Twins

B Identical twins Jim Springer and Jim Lewis were **adopted** as babies and **raised** by different couples. When the two Jims finally met at age 39, they discovered they had plenty in common. Both were 182 centimeters tall and weighed 82 kilograms. They had the same smile and the same voice. When psychologist Thomas Bouchard Jr. invited the Jim twins to his lab, his **colleagues** found it very hard to **tell** them **apart**.

C But the similarities didn't stop at the physical. They had both had dogs named Toy. They had both married women named Linda, and then **divorced** them. They had both been sheriffs,[1] enjoyed making things with wood, suffered **severe** headaches, and **admitted** to leaving love notes around the house for their wives. They had so much in common that it seemed unlikely these were just **coincidences**.

Genetics and Intelligence

D The Jim twins were just one of 137 sets of separated twins Bouchard tested. When they compared the twins' IQ scores, Bouchard and his team reached a surprising conclusion. They concluded that intelligence was mostly connected to genetics rather than to training or education. It seemed the differences in family and environment had little effect.

E However, genes can't control everything, argues geneticist Danielle Reed, who also studies twins. Reed's research shows that, though nothing can truly change our DNA, environmental differences that a child experiences before birth and in their first year can sometimes affect the way the DNA behaves. This can make even identical twins into vastly different people. "What I like to say is that Mother Nature[2] writes some things in pencil and some things in pen," she explains. "Things written in pen you can't change. That's DNA. But things written in pencil you can."

∧ Placed side by side, the Jim twins' faces (Lewis on the left, Springer on the right) are so alike that they seem to make a single face.

---

1 A **sheriff** is a kind of police officer.
2 **Mother Nature** is sometimes used to refer to nature, especially when it is being considered as a force that affects human beings.

A. Choose the best answer for each question.

GIST

1. What is the reading mainly about?

    a. how identical twins are formed

    b. the effects genes have on personality

    c. the differences between identical twins

DETAIL

2. In the past, scientists believed that _____.

    a. genetics only controlled our appearance

    b. genetics controlled everything about who we are

    c. our genes are affected by the environment around us

REFERENCE

3. Who does the word *they* refer to in the second sentence of paragraph D?

    a. the Jim Twins

    b. sets of twins

    c. Bouchard and his team

∧ **Identical twins, like these young surfers, often share the same hobbies.**

DETAIL

4. According to Bouchard and his team, what is intelligence mostly related to?

    a. genetics

    b. education

    c. parenting

VOCABULARY

5. In paragraph E, the word *vastly* is closest in meaning to _____.

    a. unfortunately

    b. interestingly

    c. extremely

SUMMARIZING

B. Complete the summary. Choose the correct options (a–f). One is extra.

a. birth	b. DNA	c. levels of intelligence
d. physical similarities	e. the environment	f. their meeting

In the past, scientists who studied identical twins thought that [1]_____ were genetic, but other differences, such as personality and intelligence, were caused by [2]_____. Recent studies show that it is not quite as simple as that. A study by Thomas Bouchard suggests that [3]_____ are more closely linked to genetics than training or education. However, Danielle Reed's research suggests that the behavior of [4]_____ can be affected by the environment, both before [5]_____ and in a child's first year.

Making Inferences

A reading text does not always state everything directly. Sometimes you need to "read between the lines" to find—or infer—the meaning. You can infer meaning by using your knowledge of the topic, clues and hints in the text, and common sense. An inference is a kind of "smart guess." Making inferences while reading allows the reader to reach a deeper level of meaning.

MAKING
INFERENCES

A. Look back at paragraphs B–D of Reading B. Then read the sentences below about the Jim twins. Can you infer the information below from the information given in the passage? Circle **Yes** or **No**.

1. The Jim twins have similar personalities.	**Yes**	**No**
2. The Jim twins both have sons but no daughters.	**Yes**	**No**
3. Bouchard gave the Jim twins an IQ test.	**Yes**	**No**
4. The Jim twins got divorced for similar reasons.	**Yes**	**No**
5. In Bouchard's study, most people tested had a similar IQ level to their twin.	**Yes**	**No**

MAKING
INFERENCES

B. Use information inferred from the reading passage and your own knowledge to answer the questions below. Check (✓) the option that best matches your opinion.

1. Do you think studies like Bouchard's are common?

☐ definitely   ☐ probably   ☐ probably not   ☐ definitely not

2. Do you think the Jim twins grew up in very different environments?

☐ definitely   ☐ probably   ☐ probably not   ☐ definitely not

3. Do you think geneticists often study identical twins?

☐ definitely   ☐ probably   ☐ probably not   ☐ definitely not

4. Do you think similarities in the Jim twins' lifestyles were mainly coincidences?

☐ definitely   ☐ probably   ☐ probably not   ☐ definitely not

CRITICAL THINKING Justifying Opinions   Explain the reasons for your answers in activity B. What information in the reading passage informed your opinion? Make notes below and then discuss with a partner.

_____

_____

_____

COMPLETION   **A.** Complete the information using the words in the box. One word is extra.

admitted	adopted	apart
boundaries	coincidences	raised

In 2013, Samantha Futerman—an actress in the United States—received a Facebook message that changed her life. The message was from Anais Bordier, a young woman from France. She told Samantha that she had been ¹_____ as a baby, and thought Samantha could be her twin. When Samantha saw Anais, she ²_____ that they did look very similar. In fact, it was almost impossible to tell them ³_____. The young women found out that they had been born on the same date in the same town in South Korea, and had very similar personalities. To confirm that these weren't just ⁴_____, they took DNA tests, which concluded that they were identical twins. ⁵_____ by different families in different countries, neither had known she had a sister.

The film *Twinsters*—about how Futerman and Bordier discovered they were twins—was released in 2015.

DEFINITIONS   **B.** Complete the sentences. Circle the correct options.

1. If a disease is **genetic**, *your friends / others in your family* are likely to have it.

2. If you have a **severe** pain in your leg, it hurts *a lot / a little*.

3. The **boundaries** of a country are at the *edges / center* of its land.

4. If your parents are **divorced**, they are no longer *alive / married*.

5. Your **colleagues** are people you *live / work* with.

COLLOCATIONS   **C.** The nouns in the box are often used with the word **severe**. Complete the sentences using the correct form of the words in the box.

headache	injury	problem	weather

1. Unemployment is becoming a severe _____ in this country.

2. Fortunately, the accident didn't cause any severe _____.

3. Severe _____ conditions have been forecast for the coming week.

4. If you have a severe _____, it's best to go and lie down in a dark room.

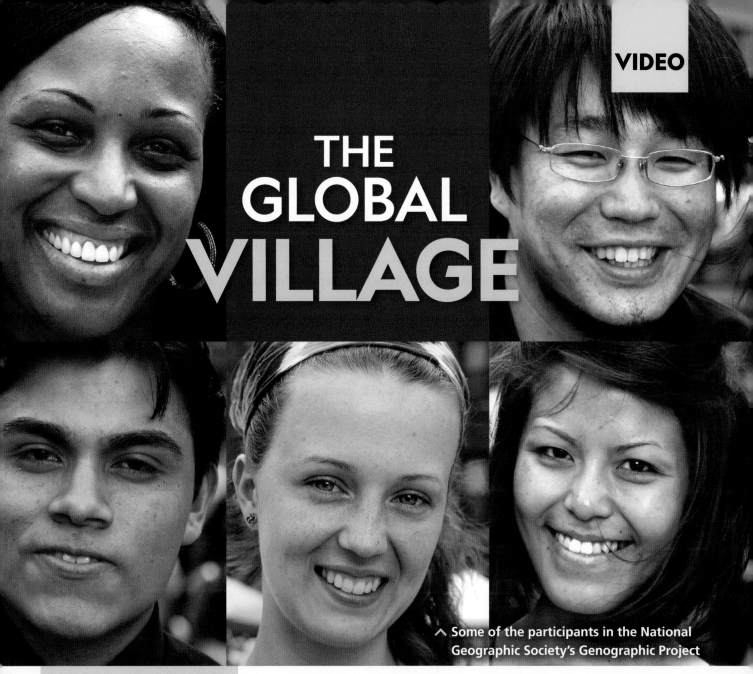

VIDEO

THE GLOBAL VILLAGE

∧ **Some of the participants in the National Geographic Society's Genographic Project**

DISCUSSION **A.** Look at the photos and read the information below about the Genographic Project. Then note answers to the questions and discuss with a partner.

Since 2005, the National Geographic Society's Genographic Project has worked to answer important questions about who we are as human beings, like: *Where did humans come from? How did we come to live all over the Earth?* The project collects DNA from people all around the world and studies it to see what has been passed down from their ancestors. The results provide valuable information about our past.

1. What are some places that people in your country originally came from?

_____

2. What are some possible benefits of learning about our past from our DNA?

_____

GIST **A.** Watch the video. Complete the sentences by circling the correct options.

1. The participants are grouped according to where *their ancestors came from /
they were born*.

2. Participants are taken on a journey *back / forwards* in time.

3. In the end, all the participants arrive in *Africa / Europe*.

COMPLETION **B.** Watch the video again. Complete the diagram using the places in the box.

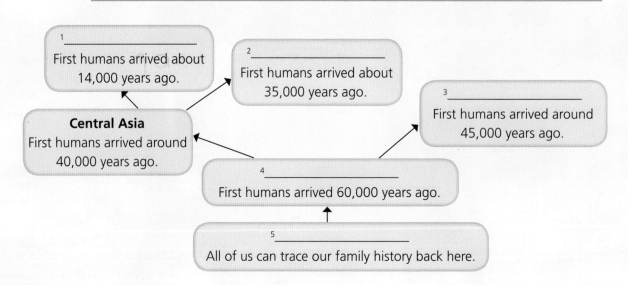

| Africa   East & South Asia   Europe   the Americas   the Middle East |

1 _____
First humans arrived about 14,000 years ago.

2 _____
First humans arrived about 35,000 years ago.

3 _____
First humans arrived around 45,000 years ago.

Central Asia
First humans arrived around 40,000 years ago.

4 _____
First humans arrived 60,000 years ago.

5 _____
All of us can trace our family history back here.

CRITICAL THINKING Reflecting   What new information did you learn from the video? Did you
find anything surprising? Note your ideas below. Then discuss with a partner.

_____

VOCABULARY REVIEW

Do you remember the meanings of these words? Check (✓) the ones you know. Look back at the
unit and review any words you're not sure of.

Reading A

☐ conclude*   ☐ deal with   ☐ excitement   ☐ go through   ☐ intense*

☐ pleasure   ☐ realize   ☐ reward   ☐ risk   ☐ upgrade

Reading B

☐ admit   ☐ adopt   ☐ boundary   ☐ coincidence*   ☐ colleague*

☐ divorce   ☐ genetic   ☐ raise   ☐ severe   ☐ tell apart

* Academic Word List

10

FACING CHANGE

Discuss these questions with a partner.

1. What areas of the world do you think are most affected by climate change? Why?

2. Have you noticed any effects of climate change where you live?

∧ People from Uummannaq, Greenland, watch a climate change documentary projected onto an iceberg.

BEFORE YOU READ

INTERPRETING
INFOGRAPHICS

Review this
reading skill
in Unit 5A

A. Look at the map on page 146 and read the caption. Use the
information to complete the sentences below.

1. The map shows the change in global temperatures from
_____1960_____ to _____2014_____.

2. Since the late nineteenth century, average temperatures on
Earth have risen by _7.5 degrees_

3. While some areas off the coast of _antartica_ have
actually cooled, parts of the Arctic have seen temperatures rise
as much as _15°F_.

SCANNING **B.** Scan the reading and circle all the place names. Find each
place on the map on page 146. Which places have seen the
greatest rise in temperature?

THE BIG
THAW

A melting ice cap creates a waterfall in Svalbard, Norway.

A The Chacaltaya ski area sits upon a small mountain glacier in Bolivia. Although the area is less than a kilometer long, it once **hosted** international ski competitions. In the past ten years, however, the snow has melted very quickly. As the Chacaltaya glacier melts, dark rocks are uncovered. These rocks **absorb** more heat, causing temperatures to increase, so the remaining snow melts faster. The cycle seems unstoppable. Today, the snow is almost gone, and so are Chacaltaya's days as a popular ski resort.

A Global Problem

B In recent years, scientists all around the world have come to a **terrifying** conclusion. Global warming is a real problem, and one largely caused by human activity. But as experts debate how to solve the problem, ice near the North and South Poles is melting even faster than environmentalists once feared. Ten years ago, scientists warned that the Arctic Ocean could lose all its ice in about a hundred years. Now, they think it could happen much sooner. As climate scientist Mark Serreze says, "Reality is **exceeding** expectations."

Glacier Run

C The ice sheet of Greenland is also melting more quickly than scientists predicted. One of its largest glaciers, Jakobshavn Isbræ, is moving toward the sea faster than expected. In fact, the glacier is moving twice as fast as it was in 1995. Rising air and sea temperatures are two well-known causes. Researchers have also discovered other **unexpected** processes that cause glaciers to melt faster. For instance, water from melting ice runs down **cracks** in the surface and gets between the ice and rock below. This makes it easier for the glacier to **slide** into the warmer sea water.

D Some researchers believe that the melting of Greenland's ice, if it continues, could add at least a meter to global sea levels by 2100. If the ice sheet of Antarctica continues to melt at its current rate, the next few centuries could see at least a two-meter rise in sea levels, forcing tens of millions of people out of their homes.

Drying Out

E   While the melting of glaciers may flood some areas of the Earth, in other places, global warming is making water disappear. Many scientists think the glaciers of the Himalayas and the Andes could disappear in this century. As a result, millions of people in India, Bangladesh, Bolivia, and Peru—who depend on water from mountain glaciers like Chacaltaya—could find themselves in a **critical** situation. An increasing number of heat waves and droughts worldwide also suggests global warming is having an impact on humans right now, and that it could change the face of the world in the future.

F   How can we avoid these terrible **consequences**? "We all have a role to play in saving our planet," says Oscar-winning actor Leonardo DiCaprio, a producer of the documentary movie *Before the Flood,* which helped to raise awareness of the problem. DiCaprio believes that an immediate **shift** in people's attitude to climate change is needed. "We need to vote for leaders who understand the serious issues impacting our climate," he says. "There is no issue this important—because the future of the planet is at stake."

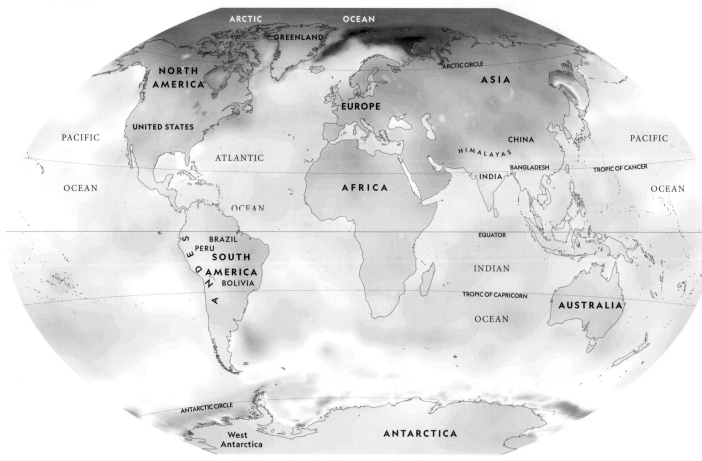

Temperature trend, 1960-2014

Change in degrees Fahrenheit

-5°   No change   +5°   +10°   +15°

Cooler   Warmer

NG STAFF
SOURCES: STEVEN MOSHER AND ROBERT ROHDE, BERKELEY EARTH

⌃ On average, the Earth has warmed 1.5 degrees Fahrenheit (0.83 degrees Celsius) since the late nineteenth century. Most of the warming has occurred since 1960.

A. Choose the best answer for each question.

MAIN IDEA

1. What is the main idea of the reading passage?

   a. The movie *Before the Flood* is raising awareness of climate change.
   b. Global warming is causing many problems on Earth.
   c. Scientists are finding ways to slow the melting of glaciers.

REASONS

2. What reason is NOT given for the faster glacier movement in Greenland?

   a. warming air temperatures
   b. unusual rainfall patterns
   c. water getting beneath the ice

DETAIL

3. What do some researchers believe will happen by the year 2100?

   a. Global sea levels will rise by at least a meter.
   b. Millions of homes will be lost in Greenland.
   c. The ice sheet of Antarctica will completely melt.

^ **The Arctic fox is one of many animals whose habitats are threatened by melting sea ice.**

INFERENCE

4. What does DiCaprio mean by "the future of the planet is at stake"?

   a. Nobody knows what the world will be like in years to come.
   b. There is a risk that the entire world could be seriously affected.
   c. There is much disagreement about how the world is changing.

MAIN IDEA

5. What would be the best heading for the final paragraph?

   a. What Can We Do?
   b. What Is the Cause?
   c. Who Is to Blame?

CAUSE AND EFFECT

Review this reading skill in Unit 6A

B. Complete the steps in the diagram describing the melting of Chacaltaya glacier. Write the correct letter (a–e) in each space.

   a. More dark rocks are uncovered.
   b. The snow melts more quickly.
   c. The Chacaltaya glacier melts.
   d. The rocks absorb more heat.
   e. The temperature rises.

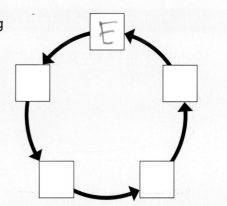

Identifying Supporting Information

When a writer makes a claim, pay attention to how the claim is supported. Look for details and examples that support the claim. Here are some different ways:

Common sense: *It's clear that …*   *Most people would agree that …*

Examples: *… such as …*   *For example / instance, …*

Facts or statistics: (general knowledge or historical) *It's a fact that this happened.* (measurements) *Fifty percent of the people …*

Informed opinion: *One expert claims …*   *According to a recent research study, …*

IDENTIFYING
SUPPORTING
DETAILS

A. The claims below are all made in Reading A. For each one, look back at the passage and underline any supporting information.

1. *Global warming is a real problem, and one largely caused by human activity.* (paragraph B)

2. *The ice sheet of Greenland is also melting more quickly than scientists predicted.* (paragraph C)

3. *Researchers have also discovered other unexpected processes that cause glaciers to melt faster.* (paragraph C)

4. *… the melting of Greenland's ice, if it continues, could add at least a meter to global sea levels by 2100.* (paragraph D)

5. *… global warming is having an impact on humans right now.* (paragraph E)

6. *… an immediate shift in people's attitude to climate change is needed.* (paragraph F)

ANALYZING

B. For each claim above, do you think the author provided enough supporting information? Why or why not? Discuss your ideas with a partner.

CRITICAL THINKING Evaluating Claims

▶ Look back at Reading A in Unit 1. Find and underline any supporting details for each claim below.

1. Our love of sugar may actually be an addiction. — Claim

2. Sugar is a major cause of high blood pressure and diabetes. — Claim

3. It's difficult to avoid sugar in today's world. — Claim

4. There are some people who are fighting back against sugar. — Claim

▶ How well supported is each claim? Discuss your ideas with a partner.

VOCABULARY PRACTICE

COMPLETION **A.** Complete the information using the words in the box. One word is extra.

Tourists visit a waterfall formed by a melting glacier.

| absorbs | consequence | critical | exceeds | terrifying |

The Arctic ice is melting quickly. As more ice disappears, the exposed ocean ¹ _absorbs_ more sunlight. As a ² _consequence_, air temperatures increase, which leads to even more melting ice. Scientists believe that eventually only a thin strip of year-round ice will remain.

This remaining ice is unlikely to be centered around the North Pole. Over the next few decades, scientists predict that winds and currents will push it to just off northern Canada. It is a ³ _terrifying_ thought, but this final area of ice may be the "last stand" for much of the Arctic's wildlife. For the few species that remain in the area, the situation will be even more ⁴ _critical_ than today.

DEFINITIONS **B.** Complete the definitions. Circle the correct options.

1. A **crack** in an object is damage in the shape of a *thin line* / *large hole*.

2. An event that is **unexpected** will probably *surprise* / *not surprise* you.

3. If you have a **shift** in your opinion, it *changes* / *becomes stronger*.

4. When something **slides** forward, it moves *smoothly* / *with difficulty*.

5. To **host** an event means to *take part in* / *provide the facilities* for it.

6. If the temperature **exceeds** 35 degrees, it is *more* / *less* than 35 degrees.

COLLOCATIONS **C.** The adjectives in **bold** below are frequently used with the noun **shift**. Complete the sentences. Circle the correct words.

1. Over time, there has been a **gradual** / **sudden** shift in people's attitudes to conservation.

2. After reading the news story, there was a **gradual** / **sudden** shift in his mood.

3. There has been a **major** / **slight** shift in how we do business. A lot of things are going to change.

4. There was only a **major** / **slight** shift in the government's environmental policy, which angered some environmentalists.

BEFORE YOU READ

PREDICTING **A.** Read the photo caption and answer these questions with a partner.

1. Where is Uummannaq? What kind of place is it?

2. How is Uummannaq different in the summer compared to the winter?

3. How do you think climate change might be affecting life in places like Uummannaq? Note some ideas.

PREVIEWING **B.** Read the passage. Which of your ideas for question 3 are mentioned?

HOTEL
UUMMANNAQ

LIFE
ON THE EDGE

A The old ways have little **appeal** for Malik Løvstrøm. A slim twenty-four-year-old, Løvstrøm has lived his whole life in Uummannaq. The people in this small town on Greenland's west coast survive mainly on seal hunting and fishing. But Løvstrøm's interests lie elsewhere—in rock music and horror movies. He taught himself English by listening to music, and now dreams of working as a tour guide on Greenland's cruise ships. He knows he should move to a larger town, as many of his friends have done. But doing so would leave no one to care for his 80-year-old grandmother. So, he remains in Uummannaq.

B Small towns all over Greenland are losing population. Niaqornat, a settlement near Uummannaq, is now home to just fifty people. The instability of towns like these has worsened as a result of climate change. Ice loss has shortened the hunting season, and as a result, traditional hunting and fishing can no longer pay for access to modern amenities.[1] Long before the sea ice disappears, **economic** and social pressures may force people to leave these settlements.

---

1 **Amenities** are useful features or facilities provided in a certain place (e.g., supermarkets, sports facilities).

∨ The town of Uummannaq, Greenland, is home to just over 1,000 people. During the summer, it is an island, but when the sea freezes, residents can use dogsleds and snowmobiles for hunting trips and visits to other islands.

C   The question of what to do about this problem is a common topic of **debate** at gatherings known as *kaffemik*. At one community **gathering**, Jean-Michel Huctin, a French anthropologist,[2] gets into a lively discussion with a man who has moved to Nuuk, Greenland's largest town. The subject is the future of places like Niaqornat—and whether they even have one.

D   "If we don't move out of isolation, we will always be conservative,"[3] the man from Nuuk tells Huctin. "I don't want to live in a museum. I don't want to live in the old way. My son, my daughter should be part of the world." The traditional **lifestyles** survive only because of **government** subsidies,[4] he argues. This approach forces young people into a life of hunting and fishing rather than **encouraging** them to look beyond tradition.

---

2 An **anthropologist** is someone who studies people and society.

3 If someone is **conservative**, they prefer not to make big changes.

4 A **subsidy** is money given, usually by a government, to help a certain business or industry.

When Albert Lukassen was young, he could hunt by dogsled on Uummannaq's frozen waters until June. This photo shows him there in April.

E But job opportunities in Greenland are few, Huctin counters. Anyway, what would happen to the older hunters? Should they **give up** their independence—their boats and dogsleds—and live in a city apartment building? The loss of settlements would be a loss for all, he says. Such places preserve Inuit hunting culture. But Huctin is hopeful: "I think these small, remote communities can invent a sustainable future for themselves," he says. "The people have gone from hunting to Facebook in less than a century ... I'm sure they will succeed in the future."

F Fewer people are choosing to stay, however; even fewer arrive from outside. An **exception** is Ilannguaq Egede, who moved to Niaqornat to be with his girlfriend. His first job was cleaning the town's toilets, but now he **manages** the town's power plant. "I like it here a lot," he says. "I have a home and a nice salary. You can feel the freshness here, and it's open," he says. "I don't want to move anyplace else."

A. Choose the best answer for each question.

GIST

1. What is the reading mainly about?

a. problems facing small towns in Greenland
b. how people in Greenland still hunt for food
c. the rising populations of Greenland's major cities

DETAIL

2. Which of the following is NOT true about Uummannaq?

a. It is the largest town in Greenland.
b. Most people there follow a traditional lifestyle.
c. Climate change is affecting the economy.

DETAIL

3. According to information in paragraph A, Malik Løvstrøm's ambition is to _____.

a. hunt seals and fish
b. work in the tourism industry
c. move to another country

VOCABULARY

4. In paragraph D, what does the word *isolation* mean?

a. separation
b. tradition
c. community

△ **A group of people from Uummannaq walk across the frozen sea.**

PURPOSE

5. The author refers to Ilannguaq Egede in paragraph F to indicate that _____.

a. there are no good jobs available in small towns in Greenland
b. not everyone is preparing to move away from small settlements in Greenland
c. at least one person still wants to be a traditional hunter or fisher

SUMMARIZING

B. Complete the sentences using the correct ending (a–g). Two endings are extra.

a. job opportunities	b. ice loss	c. independence
d. modern amenities	e. government subsidies	f. community gatherings
g. population loss		

1. The hunting season in Greenland is not as long as it used to be due to __b__.

2. The man from Nuuk believes that traditional hunting and fishing would disappear without __g__.

3. Without their boats and sleds, older hunters and fishers would not have their __d__.

4. According to the French anthropologist, Greenland has a lack of __b__.

5. Traditional hunters and fishers can no longer afford __c__.

Identifying Arguments For and Against an Issue

Writers often present two sides of an argument—giving reasons for and against an idea. To identify and evaluate both sides of an argument, it can be useful to take notes in a T-chart, summarizing the arguments for and against in different columns.

IDENTIFYING ARGUMENTS **A.** Which paragraph outlines the argument for why people should move out of places such as Niaqornat? ____
Which outlines the argument for why people should remain there? ____

UNDERSTANDING ARGUMENTS **B.** Complete the notes in the chart using words from the reading passage. Use up to three words for each blank.

Issue: Should people in Greenland leave traditional settlements and move to other parts of the country?	
Arguments for:	**Arguments against:**
• These settlements are ¹_____ from the rest of the world. • They only survive because of money from the ²_____. • Young people can only find traditional jobs like ³_____ and ⁴_____.	• There are not many ⁵_____ in other parts of Greenland. • It would be difficult for hunters to adapt to life in a(n) ⁶_____. • The settlements preserve ⁷_____. • The communities should be able to change and have a(n) ⁸_____.

CRITICAL THINKING Analyzing Arguments

▶ Look again at the arguments in the chart above. Do you think one argument is stronger than the other? Do you think the arguments are well-balanced? Discuss with a partner.

▶ Imagine you are a young resident of Uummannaq. Would you choose to stay or leave? Note your ideas below. Then discuss with a partner.

_____

_____

_____

_____

COMPLETION **A.** Complete the information using the correct form of the words in the box.

appeal	economic	encourage
give up	government	lifestyle

It's not only Arctic communities that are facing problems caused by climate change. The people of Kiribati, a group of islands in the Pacific Ocean, are also seeing their land slowly disappear. Much of Tarawa, Kiribati's capital, is less than two meters above sea level and risks being flooded as the ocean rises. Kiribati's ¹ _government_ has ² _appealed_ for international help, and the island has received foreign aid and other ³ _economic_ support. This has ⁴ _encouraged_ many of the islanders to stay, for now. Eventually, however, the people of Kiribati will likely have to move to another country. They are determined, though, not to lose their unique culture and ⁵ _lifestyle_ —even if they have to ⁶ _give up_ their land to the sea.

An aerial view of the Kiribati island Kiritimati

DEFINITIONS **B.** Match the two parts of each definition.

1. If you have a **gathering**, •   • a. you discuss an issue with other people.

2. If you have a **debate**, •   • b. you treat something differently than everything else.

3. If you make an **exception**, •   • c. you control it.

4. If you **manage** a business, •   • d. you meet with a group of people.

COLLOCATIONS **C.** Many phrasal verbs use the preposition *up*, such as **give up**. Complete the sentences using the words in the box. One word is extra.

keep	make	set	show	take

1. People often _take_ up a new hobby at the start of a new year.

2. Novel writers need to be able to _make_ up interesting stories.

3. It's important to _show_ up on time for a job interview.

4. It's sometimes hard to _keep_ up with the latest technology.

THE SLED DOGS OF GREENLAND

A team of sled dogs pull their owner across the ice in Ilulissat, Greenland.

BEFORE YOU WATCH

PREVIEWING **A.** Read the information. The words in **bold** appear in the video. Complete the definitions (1–4) by circling the correct words.

In places like Greenland, Alaska, and Norway—where the **landscape** is covered with snow and ice for months at a time—people have always used sleds pulled by teams of tough dogs. **Descended** from wolves, these sled dogs help people travel out across the ice to hunt and fish. They are fierce enough to confront polar bears, and strong enough to pull hundreds of kilograms across the snow. However, the sled dogs need a lot of food and care, and owning a team can be a great **expense**. And, as global warming melts away the ice, sled dogs are becoming less of a **necessity**.

1. An **expense** is something that *costs* / *makes* money.
2. If something is a **necessity**, you *need* / *don't need* it.
3. You are **descended** from *your brothers and sisters* / *family that lived in the past*.
4. A beautiful **landscape** might include *mountains and rivers* / *people and vehicles*.

GIST **A.** Watch the video. Complete the sentences by circling the correct words.

1. Compared to other dogs, Greenland's sled dogs are *a new /* (*an old* breed.)
2. *Fewer /* (*More*) fishermen in Greenland now use boats.
3. In Ilulissat, there are *fewer /* (*only slightly*) more people than sled dogs.
4. Marit Holm needs to take care because (*the dogs sometimes bite /* the ice is very thin.)
5. The Greenland government is helping by (*making new laws /* retraining the dogs.)

SUMMARIZING **B.** Watch the video again. Complete the sentences about Finn Sistall and Marit Holm. Use one or two words.

1. Finn Sistall works as a ___fisherman___. When he was young, his family had a ___team___ of 19 sled dogs. Eventually, they weren't needed anymore because there is far less ___ice___ in Greenland.

2. Marit Holm works as a ___vet___. Every day she drives around town looking for sled dogs that ___are sick___. She also teaches owners how to ___take care___ of their dogs.

CRITICAL THINKING Inferring Information

▶ Discuss with a partner. What laws do you think the Greenland government passed to help the sled dogs?

▶ What else could be done to help Greenland's unwanted sled dogs? Note some ideas. Then discuss with a partner.

VOCABULARY REVIEW

Do you remember the meanings of these words? Check (✓) the ones you know. Look back at the unit and review any words you're not sure of.

Reading A

☐ absorb   ☐ consequence*   ☐ crack   ☐ critical   ☐ exceed*

☐ host   ☐ shift*   ☐ slide   ☐ terrifying   ☐ unexpected

Reading B

☐ appeal   ☐ debate*   ☐ economic* ☐ encourage   ☐ exception

☐ gathering   ☐ give up   ☐ government ☐ lifestyle   ☐ manage

* Academic Word List

11

FACT OR FAKE?

A. ALICE AND THE FAIRIES

⌃ In 1917, two young girls from Cottingley, England, released a set of photographs supposedly showing fairies they had seen in their garden. The images were fake—the fairies were simply paper cutouts—but people around the world believed the Cottingley Fairies were real. In 2018, the original photos sold at auction for over $25,000.

BEFORE YOU READ

PREVIEWING **A.** Read the question below and quickly note your answer.

A bat and a ball cost $1.10 in total. The bat costs $1.00 more than the ball. How much does the ball cost? _____

SCANNING **B.** Compare your answer with a partner. Then scan the reading passage to check if you were correct.

SKIMMING **C.** Skim the rest of the reading. What answer do most people give? Why?

THE KNOWLEDGE
ILLUSION

A A bat and a ball cost $1.10 in total. The bat costs $1.00 more than the ball. How much does the ball cost?

B If you answered 10 cents, you're not alone—most people give the same answer (the correct answer is 5 cents). It's an example of how we often **rely on** intuitive responses—answers we feel are true. People give answers that "pop into their mind," says cognitive scientist[1] Steven Sloman. We don't spend much time "reflecting and checking whether the answer … is right or wrong."

C The bat and ball question helps explain why we often believe in fake news. It is part of human nature to believe, says Sloman. But "the trick with fake news is to know to verify"—in other words, to stop and question what you know.

D In one **experiment**, Sloman and a colleague invented a discovery called helium[2] rain. They told a group of **volunteers** about it, but admitted they could not fully explain what it was. They then asked the volunteers to rate their own understanding of helium rain. Most volunteers rated themselves 1 out of 7, meaning they did not understand the **concept**.

E The **researchers** then told another group of volunteers about the discovery. This time, they said that scientists could fully explain how it works. When asked to rate their understanding, the volunteers gave an **average** answer of 2. The scientists' confidence gave the volunteers an increased sense of their own understanding, Sloman says.

⌄ **A 3-D street painting in Dún Laoghaire, Ireland, creates an amazing illusion.**

---

1 A **cognitive scientist** studies the processes in the brain related to knowing, learning, and understanding.
2 **Helium** is a very light, colorless gas.

F According to Sloman, studies show that knowledge spreads like a contagion.[3] This idea can be seen in many fields, including politics. "If everyone around you is saying they understand why a politician is crooked,"[4] Sloman says, "then you're going to start thinking that you understand, too."

G Another explanation for the spread of fake news is "motivated reasoning," writes Adam Waytz, a management professor at the Kellogg School. We are naturally more likely to believe things that confirm our existing opinions. If you already have a negative opinion about someone, you're more likely to trust damaging stories about them. Over time, Waytz argues, "motivated reasoning can lead to a false social consensus."[5]

H So, in a world where misleading information is common, is there a way to protect ourselves? "I don't think it's possible to train **individuals** to verify everything that they **encounter**," Sloman admits. "It is just too human to believe what you're told."

I However, training people to care about fact-checking is important, he argues, especially in online communities. Think of the headlines and stories that are shared on your social **media** feed every day. Probably these fit in with your own worldview—but perhaps not all of them are true.

J "Develop a **norm** in your community that says, 'We should check things and not just take them at face value,'" Sloman says. "Verify before you believe."

---

3 A **contagion** is a disease that spreads easily.

4 If someone is described as **crooked**, they are dishonest.

5 A **social consensus** refers to a group of people sharing the same opinions.

⌃ A mirror illusion at a fair in Dallas, United States

A. Choose the best answer for each question.

GIST

1. What would be the best alternative title for the reading?

   a. Helium Rain: A Great Discovery
   b. Stop, Question, and Verify
   c. Social Media and How to Use It

VOCABULARY

2. In paragraph C, what does the word *verify* mean?

   a. to make sure something is true
   b. to think about something for a long time
   c. to express an opinion about something

PURPOSE

3. The author uses the example of the bat and ball question to show that ____.

   a. people often forget skills that they learned at school
   b. there is often more than one possible answer to a question
   c. many people give quick responses without thinking carefully

DETAIL

4. More volunteers claimed to understand helium rain when ____.

   a. some of the volunteers explained it to them
   b. Sloman and his colleagues showed them how it works
   c. they believed that scientists fully understood it

INFERENCE

5. Which of the following is an example of "motivated reasoning"?

   a. You are not sure a story on social media is true, so you search online for more information.
   b. You post a message online that gives your opinion about a news story.
   c. You don't believe a negative story about a soccer player because he plays for your favorite team.

EVALUATING STATEMENTS

B. Are the following statements true or false according to the reading passage, or is the information not given? Circle **T** (true), **F** (false), or **NG** (not given).

1. Sloman and his colleagues discovered helium rain. **T F NG**

2. The volunteers were told that helium rain comes from certain clouds. **T F NG**

3. The second group of volunteers rated their understanding of helium rain higher than the first. **T F NG**

4. Waytz has carried out many experiments to investigate "motivated reasoning." **T F NG**

Dealing with Unfamiliar Vocabulary (3)—Using a Dictionary

If you are unable to guess the meaning of an unfamiliar word from context, you may want to check in a dictionary. When doing so, remember the following:

- Some words have the same spelling but different meanings. Use the context to help identify the most relevant meaning, as well as the correct part of speech.

- Check if the word is part of a longer phrase. If it is, checking the meaning of the individual word may not be helpful. In a good dictionary, you will be able to search for whole phrases.

For example, the word *pop* appears in Reading A, paragraph B: *People give answers that "pop into their mind"* . . .

If you check this word in a dictionary, you may find the following definitions:
pop (n) modern music that is liked by many people
pop (v) to make or cause to make a short sharp sound

From context, we can guess that neither definition is correct. In this case, *pop* is part of a longer phrase "pop into their mind." By searching for the full phrase, you can find the correct definition:
pop into your mind (phr): If something pops into your mind, you suddenly think about it.

SCANNING

A. Look back at Reading A and scan for the words below. Use context to check the correct meaning of each word as it is used in the passage. Circle the correct definition.

1. **rate** (paragraph D)
   a. *rate* (n) the speed at which something happens
   b. *rate* (v) to decide how good or bad something is
   c. *at any rate* (phr) anyway

2. **lead** (paragraph G)
   a. *lead* (v) to control a group of people
   b. *lead to* (v) to cause
   c. *lead* (n) a piece of wire covered in plastic

3. **feed** (paragraph I)
   a. *feed* (v) to give food
   b. *feed into* (v) to put into
   c. *feed* (n) the way information is displayed on social media

SCANNING

B. Scan for the following words and check them in a dictionary. Write a definition for each word as it is used in the reading passage.

nature (paragraph C): _____

train (paragraph H): _____

face (paragraph J): _____

VOCABULARY PRACTICE

COMPLETION   **A.** Complete the information using the words and phrases in the box.

average   concept   encounter   media   norm   rely on

As human beings, we ¹_____ other people for most of the knowledge that we learn. We gain so much from believing others that if we occasionally believe a lie, there is relatively little harm. Most people therefore have a tendency to trust others. However, this results in what psychologist Robert Feldman calls "the liar's advantage." According to this ²_____, the ³_____ person does not expect to hear lies, and the ⁴_____ is to believe what you hear. This is one reason why people tend to believe false information that they ⁵_____ on social ⁶_____.

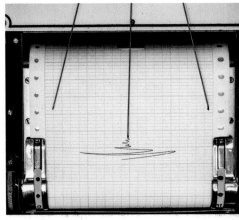

∧ **Polygraph machines—or lie detectors—work by measuring physical signs of lying, such as blood pressure and heartbeat.**

DEFINITIONS   **B.** Match the two parts of each definition.

1. An **experiment** •   • a. is someone who offers to do a particular task.
2. A **researcher** •   • b. is a scientific test.
3. A **volunteer** •   • c. is a single person.
4. An **individual** •   • d. is a person who finds out information.

COLLOCATIONS   **C.** The nouns in the box are frequently used with the adjective **average**. Complete the sentences using the correct word.

day   size   family   salary

1. The average _____ in my country is around $60,000 per year.

2. On an average _____, I use social media for around three hours.

3. The government's new tax will cost the average _____ an extra $1,000 a year.

4. In many countries, the average _____ of a new apartment is getting smaller.

BEFORE YOU READ

DISCUSSION **A.** What kinds of lies do you think are OK to tell? Why? Discuss with a partner.

SKIMMING **B.** Skim the reading passage. What was the aim of the Matrix Experiments?

    a. to understand the most common lies people tell

    b. to find out how much people will lie

    c. to study how lying develops in children

> A soccer referee shouts at a player he believes is faking injury.

THE LIMITS OF LYING

Lying is a part of human nature. But how far will people go?

A Psychologist Dan Ariely became interested in dishonesty about 15 years ago. During a long-distance flight, he came across an IQ test in a magazine. He answered the first question and checked the answer key to see if he got it right. He then took a quick look at the next answer before looking back at the quiz. He continued in this way through the whole test. Not surprisingly, he scored very well. "When I finished, I thought—I **cheated** myself," he says. So why did he do it? "**Presumably**, I wanted to know how smart I am, but I also wanted to prove I'm this smart to myself." The experience led Ariely to develop a lifelong interest in the study of lying and other forms of dishonesty.

B To find out more about lying habits, Ariely developed a series of studies known as the Matrix Experiments. In the experiments, volunteers completed a test with 20 simple math problems. They were given five minutes to solve as many as they could. For each correct answer, they were told they would receive a **sum** of money. When the time was up, the volunteers counted the number of problems they solved correctly. They were then asked to destroy their answer sheets in a shredder.[1] After **reporting** their own test **scores**, they were paid accordingly. However, there was something the volunteers didn't know. Their answer sheets were never actually destroyed.

C By comparing actual test scores to reported scores, Ariely's research team found out how many volunteers **lied**, and how much they lied by. The results? Of the 40,000 people who **participated** in the experiment, nearly 70 percent lied about their test score. On average, volunteers said they solved six problems, but it was closer to four. The results are similar across different cultures. Most of us lie, but only a little.

D The question Ariely finds most interesting is not why so many of us lie, but rather why we don't lie a lot more. In one version of the experiment, participants were offered significantly more money for each correct answer. However, this did not cause them to cheat more. "Here we give people a chance to steal lots of money, and people cheat only a little bit. So something stops us—most of us—from not lying all the way," Ariely says.

E The reason, he believes, is that we want to see ourselves as **honest**, because honesty is a value taught to us by society. This is why most of us place limits on how much we lie. We may be able to come up with an **excuse** for taking Post-it Notes[2] from an office fairly easily. "But it is much more difficult to come up with an excuse for taking $10,000," Ariely explains. The extent of our lying is determined largely by what is acceptable by society. "Cheating is easier," he says, "when we can **justify** our behavior."

---

1 A **shredder** is a machine that tears paper into thin pieces.

2 **Post-it Notes** are small pieces of paper that are sticky on one side.

A. Choose the best answer for each question.

DETAIL

1. Why did Dan Ariely first become interested in researching dishonesty?

a. He saw someone cheating on a test.
b. He looked at the answers for a quiz he was taking.
c. He lied to another passenger on an airplane.

DETAIL

2. Which of the following is true about the Matrix Experiments?

a. Volunteers who lied about their score received no money.
b. The volunteers' answer sheets were destroyed.
c. The average volunteer solved four problems correctly.

REFERENCE

3. What does *They* refer to in the third sentence of paragraph B?

a. problems
b. researchers
c. volunteers

DETAIL

4. The version of the Matrix Experiment described in paragraph D involved ____.

a. more money for correct answers
b. volunteers from different cultures
c. more than 20 problems

△ **Psychologist Dan Ariely**

SUMMARIZING

5. Which of the following statements best summarizes the conclusion Ariely draws in paragraph E?

a. Stealing office equipment is more common than stealing money.
b. Most people in a society believe themselves to be honest.
c. We learn from society what kind of lies are acceptable.

MATCHING PARAGRAPHS

B. Match the headings below to paragraphs in the reading passage (A–E). One heading is extra.

____ **1.** Why people put limits on lying

____ **2.** Contrasting ideas about dishonesty

____ **3.** The design of Ariely's experiments

____ **4.** Why Ariely chose to study lying

____ **5.** What Ariely finds most interesting about dishonesty

____ **6.** The results of the Matrix Experiments

Understanding a Research Summary

When writers describe an experiment or a piece of research, they often cover the following points:

- the **purpose** of the study (the question they want to answer)
- the **method** (how they set up and carried out the study)
- the **results** (what the study found)
- the **conclusion** (the significance of the results)

When reading a research summary, highlighting these points and noting them in the margin can help your understanding. Note that the order in which the information is presented will not always be the same.

UNDERSTANDING
RESEARCH

A. The following excerpts are from Reading B. What does each one describe? Write **purpose**, **method**, **results**, or **conclusion**.

1. Most of us lie, but only a little. _____

2. Of the 40,000 people who participated in the experiment, nearly 70 percent lied about their test score. On average, volunteers said they solved six problems, but it was closer to four. _____

3. In the experiments, volunteers completed a test with 20 simple math problems. They were given five minutes to solve as many as they could. For each correct answer, they were told they would receive a sum of money. _____

4. To find out more about lying habits, Ariely developed a series of studies known as the Matrix Experiments. _____

UNDERSTANDING
ARGUMENTS

B. Look back at Unit 2, Reading B. Highlight and label the parts of the passage that explain the purpose, method, results, and conclusion. Is the order of the information the same or different from Reading 11B?

CRITICAL THINKING Evaluating a Claim

▶ Ariely says, "Cheating is easier when we can justify our behavior." Look at the situations below. How might each person justify their behavior? Discuss your ideas with a partner.

1. A soccer player pretends to be injured even though he is fine.

2. A worker takes home some office stationery to use at home.

3. A salesperson sells a product that he knows isn't very good.

▶ List some other examples of common dishonest behavior. For each example, do you think the behavior can be justified? Discuss with a partner.

COMPLETION   **A.** Complete the information with the correct form of the words in the box.

excuse	honest	lie	participate	report

To study the development of lying in children, psychologist Kang Lee uses a simple experiment. Children who ¹_____ in the study play a simple guessing game. A card with a number on it is laid facedown on the table. The child must try to guess the number, and if they guess correctly, they win a prize. The researcher then makes a(n) ²_____ to leave the room. Hidden cameras show that most children can't stop themselves from looking at the next card. When the researcher returns, they ask the child, "Did you look at the card?" Among two-year-olds who peeked, two-thirds were ³_____ about it. But by age four, the researchers ⁴_____ that more than 80 percent of children who looked at the card lied to cover it up. The results of the experiment suggest that as children get older, they ⁵_____ more often.

DEFINITIONS   **B.** Match each word with its definition.

1. **justify**   •   • a. (n) an amount (e.g., of money)

2. **presumably** •   • b. (n) a result; e.g., in a test or game

3. **score**   •   • c. (v) to break the rules, e.g., in a game

4. **cheat**   •   • d. (adv) not certainly, but very likely

5. **sum**   •   • e. (v) to give a reason for an action

WORD FORMS   **C.** The box below shows the different forms of the word **honest**. Complete the sentences using the words in the box.

honest (adj)	honestly (adv)	honesty (n)
dishonest (adj)	dishonestly (adv)	dishonesty (n)

1. The children were punished for their _____ behavior.

2. I _____ don't know what happened to the last piece of cake.

3. Parents shouldn't encourage _____, but learning to lie is part of a child's development.

4. It was a(n) _____ mistake. I didn't mean to do it.

⌄ **A fake smile and a real smile. Can you tell which is which?**

SMILE TRIAL

BEFORE YOU WATCH

PREVIEWING **A.** Read the information. The words and phrases in **bold** appear in the video. Match the words and phrases to their definitions.

When it comes to **spotting** lies and untruths, paying attention to **nonverbal** forms of communication can be very important. Body language and **facial expressions** often give clues that someone might be lying. Blinking quickly, touching your face, and excessive sweating are all thought to be signs that someone is being dishonest. It's also possible to tell if someone is displaying **genuine** emotions. For example, if someone is smiling, but they're actually unhappy, the muscles in the face will behave slightly differently.

1. facial expression ●   ● a. to find or identify

2. genuine ●   ● b. without speaking

3. nonverbal ●   ● c. real, not fake

4. spot ●   ● d. a way of showing your emotions

PREDICTING **B.** Look at the pictures above. Which of these smiles do you think is real? Which is fake? Discuss with a partner and explain your reasons.

WHILE YOU WATCH

GIST **A.** Watch the video. Check your predictions and reasons in Before You Watch B.

DETAIL **B.** Watch the video again. Does each statement below describe a real or a fake smile? Circle the correct options.

    1. involves the movement of muscles around the eyes   **Real**   **Fake**

    2. also known as a "Duchenne smile"   **Real**   **Fake**

    3. created by Duchenne using electricity to move the muscles   **Real**   **Fake**

    4. connected to the area of the brain related to emotion   **Real**   **Fake**

    5. connected to a part of the brain called "the motor cortex"   **Real**   **Fake**

CRITICAL THINKING Applying Ideas

▶ Look at the emotions below. What body language and/or facial expressions do people use to express each one? Discuss with a partner.

anger	disappointment	interest	joy	surprise

▶ In what situations might someone want to fake the emotions above? Which are the hardest to fake? Why? Discuss with a partner and note your ideas.

_____

_____

VOCABULARY REVIEW

Do you remember the meanings of these words? Check (✓) the ones you know. Look back at the unit and review any words you're not sure of.

Reading A

☐ average   ☐ concept*   ☐ encounter*   ☐ experiment   ☐ individual

☐ media*   ☐ norm*   ☐ rely on*   ☐ researcher*   ☐ volunteer

Reading B

☐ cheat   ☐ excuse   ☐ honest   ☐ justify*   ☐ lie

☐ participate*   ☐ presumably*   ☐ report   ☐ score   ☐ sum*

* Academic Word List

GOING TO EXTREMES

12

< A climber dangles from a mountain in Antarctica.

WARM UP

Discuss these questions with a partner.

1. Where are the most extreme places a person might visit?

2. What are some of the most adventurous activities and sports you know? Which ones would you like to try?

BEFORE YOU READ

DISCUSSION **A.** What are some different ways that humans can experience flying? Work with a partner and make a list. Which of these activities have you tried? Which would you like to try? Why?

SKIMMING **B.** Skim the reading and look at the photos. What methods of flying are mentioned? What kind of flight does the author experience?

THE DREAM OF FLIGHT

by Nancy Shute

A For thousands of years, humans have dreamed of taking to the skies. The ancient Greeks told the legend of Icarus, a boy who flies so high that the sun melts his man-made **wings** and he crashes down to Earth. Across history, many more people have died after jumping from a tower or **cliff** with wings that didn't quite work. Flying, for humans, seemed an impossibility.

B Yet many continued to dream of flying. One such dreamer was the great 15th-century artist and inventor Leonardo da Vinci. He studied the flight of birds and even designed his own flying machines, but they—and he—never left the ground.

C Five hundred years later, standing on a windy hill in North Carolina, in the United States, I was about to make the dream come true.

D **Unlike** Leonardo, I had the help of a hang glider—a light, modern machine that makes flying simple and safe enough even for tourist entertainment. I held on to the hang glider as **tightly** as I could. Terrified, I ran down the hill, and suddenly, I was running in the air. I was flying! What a **thrill**! Now I wanted more.

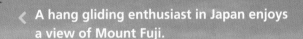

A hang gliding enthusiast in Japan enjoys a view of Mount Fuji.

Yves Rossy's two-meter-long wings allow him to fly at speeds of around 200 kilometers an hour.

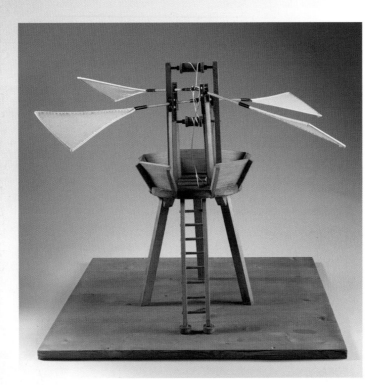

A model of a
flying machine
designed by
Leonardo da Vinci

E A friend in my hang gliding class suggested I next try a "tandem flight"—
flying in a hang glider made for two people. A small airplane carries you up
600 meters and then lets you go. I decided to try it with my instructor, Jon
Thompson. Up into the air we went. When the airplane released us, it felt like
falling from a building, headfirst. "You can fly now," my instructor said. After
a few moments, I found the **courage** to turn the glider a little to the left, and
then a little to the right. I was more like a pigeon[1] than an eagle,[2] but I was
flying!

F Of course, hang gliding is not the only way mankind has learned to enjoy the
freedom of flight. Today, many people skydive, while BASE jumpers—those
who jump off buildings, cliffs, and bridges—often get their thrills illegally. For
a few exciting moments, they experience free-falling—falling downwards with
nothing to slow them—before they open a parachute. "It's as close as human
beings can get to flying like a bird," says BASE jumper J. T. Holmes.

G Switzerland's Yves Rossy might disagree. The wings he has invented for
personal flight have four small **engines.** He **steers** them just by moving
his shoulders. For 10 minutes at a time, Rossy seems to fly as free as a bird,
having both power and control. One of his longest flights was across the
water from France to England. "It's awesome, it's great, it's **fantastic**!" says
Rossy. Since then, he has continued to improve his wing design, and hopes he
can "**motivate** the next generation of thinkers to do something different . . .
even if it seems impossible."

---

1 A **pigeon** is a common bird that usually lives in towns and cities.
2 An **eagle** is a large bird known for its strength, vision, and power of flight.

Unit 12A **177**

A. Choose the best answer for each question.

GIST

1. What is the first paragraph mainly about?

 a. why some people continue to try to fly
 b. how the Greeks were the first to try to fly
 c. how people have always dreamed of flying

DETAIL

2. How does the author describe her first hang gliding experience?

 a. terrible
 b. exciting
 c. dangerous

VOCABULARY

3. In paragraph E, what can the words *lets you go* be replaced with?

 a. allows you
 b. releases you
 c. connects you

DETAIL

4. What is NOT true about BASE jumping?

 a. Parachutes are used.
 b. People jump from airplanes.
 c. It is often illegal.

DETAIL

5. What did Yves Rossy accomplish?

 a. He invented a type of flying that doesn't use wings.
 b. He invented wings with engines that a person can wear.
 c. He flew a hang glider from France to England.

In 2013, Russia's Valery Rozov broke the record for the highest BASE jump when he jumped from a height of 7,220 meters.

SCANNING

Review this reading skill in Unit 2B

B. Scan the reading for the names below. Match each person (a–f) with the sentence that describes them. One person is extra.

a. Icarus	b. Jon Thompson	c. J. T. Holmes
d. Leonardo da Vinci	e. Nancy Shute (the author)	f. Yves Rossy

1. ＿＿ designed flying machines but never flew in one.

2. ＿＿ teaches people how to hang glide.

3. ＿＿ is a BASE jumper.

4. ＿＿ flies using a jet-powered engine.

5. ＿＿ is learning how to hang glide.

Understanding Definitions in a Text

A reading may include words that are defined in footnotes, or defined in the text itself. When a word is defined in a text, its definition may follow a comma or dash (—), or be set off by two commas or dashes. Look for these definitions as you read to better comprehend a text. Examples:

*Many smaller planes are powered by **a propeller**, <u>a device with blades that spin at high speed</u>.*
*Future planes will need less **thrust**—<u>the force from the engine that moves it forward</u>.*
***Winglets**, <u>the curved ends of an airplane's wings</u>, help planes fly more efficiently.*

ANALYZING **A. Complete the sentences using the definitions (a–f). Use a dictionary if needed.**

a. its height above the ground	d. the area where the pilot sits
b. a plane without an engine	e. a kitchen area where meals are prepared
c. the wheeled structure beneath an airplane	f. the area between the rows of seats

1. The cockpit—____—is off-limits to passengers.

2. The plane's altitude, ____, is about 55,000 km.

3. A glider, ____, cannot take off by itself.

4. On a passenger plane, the aisle—____—is kept clear at all times.

5. The undercarriage—____—is lowered just before landing.

6. Most passenger planes have a galley, ____.

SCANNING **B. Look back at Reading A. Find the words that are defined within the text and write them below.**

1. _____: a light, modern machine that makes flying simple and safe enough even for tourist entertainment

2. _____: flying in a hang glider made for two people

3. _____: those who jump off buildings, cliffs, and bridges

4. _____: falling downwards with nothing to slow them down

CRITICAL THINKING Ranking Activities   Look at the activities below. How dangerous do you think each one is? Rank them from 1–5 (1 = most dangerous). Share your reasons with a partner.

____ BASE jumping   ____ hang gliding   ____ skydiving

____ flying with a jet-powered wing   ____ flying in a small airplane

COMPLETION **A.** Complete the information using the words in the box. Two words are extra.

> **cliffs   courage   fantastic   thrill   tightly   unlike   wings**

You don't always need ¹_____
to experience the ²_____ of
flying. The United Arab Emirates has
opened a 2.8-km zipline—the world's
longest—in the emirate of Ras al-Khaimah.
The zipline allows you to soar from the
country's highest mountain peak,
gliding at speeds of 150 km/h through

∧ **A rider at the top of the Ras al-Khaimah zipline**

³_____ desert scenery, past rocky ⁴_____ and canyons, until reaching
the bottom nearly three minutes later. ⁵_____ most other ziplines, riders on
the Ras al-Khaimah zipline travel headfirst to enhance the feeling of flying.

DEFINITIONS **B.** Complete the sentences. Circle the correct options.

1. If you hold onto something **tightly**, it would be *easy / difficult* to take it from you.

2. Something that probably requires **courage** is *shopping / skydiving*.

3. A *parachute / car* has an **engine**.

4. You **steer** a car with your *hands / feet*.

5. When you **motivate** someone, you make them *stop doing / want to do* something.

WORD WEB **C.** The word **fantastic** has many synonyms. Complete the word web below with
more examples. Use a thesaurus if needed.

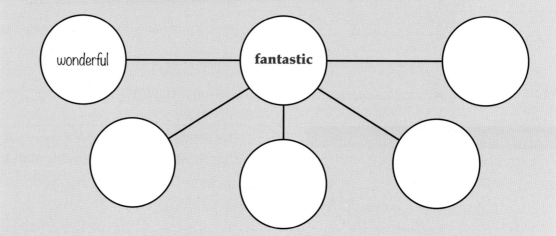

wonderful — fantastic

BEFORE YOU READ

DEFINITIONS **A.** Read the caption. Match each word in **bold** with its definition.

    1. descent •   • a. a way into a place, such as a door or an opening

    2. entrance •   • b. a movement from a higher to a lower level

    3. passage •   • c. a (usually long) space that connects two places

IDENTIFYING
DEFINITIONS

Review this
Reading Skill
in Unit 12A

B. The words below are used by cavers to describe areas in a cave. Scan the reading on the following pages and underline the definitions within the text. Then read the rest of the passage.

    squeeze (paragraph C)   **sump** (paragraph D)   **pit** (paragraph F)

< **Explorers never know what they might find as they make a descent into a cave system. Light from the cave entrance soon disappears as they move down long passages.**

DARK DESCENT

A It's August 2004. Caver Sergio García-Dils de la Vega kisses his girlfriend good-bye at the entrance of Krubera Cave. Krubera, in the western Caucasus Mountains,[1] is the deepest known cave in the world. It will be weeks before he sees her again.

B A member of an international team of 56 cavers from seven countries, García-Dils's mission was to explore Krubera. The team also hoped to be the first to reach a **depth** of 2,000 meters, a feat compared to **conquering** the North and South Poles. One team member even described descending into Krubera as "like climbing an inverted[2] mountain."

C Like climbers making their way up that famous peak, the cavers descended slowly. They climbed down ropes through huge tunnels, and crawled through tight passages known as "squeezes." Bringing over five tons[3] of equipment and other **necessities** with them, they established underground camps along the route. At each camp, they stopped to rest, eat, sleep, and plan the next part of the journey. Some days, they worked for up to 20 hours at a time. And each day, they left miles of rope behind them to **ease** their return ascent, and phone lines to communicate with people above.

Expedition members pose outside the entrance to Krubera Cave.

D In the third week, they reached 1,775 meters, the deepest point achieved by cavers so far. Here, progress was **blocked** by a sump—a passage filled with water. The cavers had only a few options: They could empty out all the water, dive through, or go around it. Gennady Samokhin dove to the bottom but was **disappointed**: "No chance to get through," he said. Searching for a way around the sump, García-Dils risked entering a cascade[4] of near-freezing water. "The water was so cold, I lost the feeling in my fingers," he said. He, too, was unsuccessful.

E Finally, the team found a way around the sump through a tight passage they called the "Way to the Dream." At first, they were thrilled**.** However, it soon led to yet another sump at 1,840 meters. After a short test dive, Samokhin **emerged**, smiling. There was a promising passage, he reported. Sadly, it would have to wait. After nearly four weeks underground, with **supplies** running low, the team was **out of time**. They would have to return to the surface.

F Four weeks later, following the path opened by García-Dils's team, a team of Ukrainian cavers reached the sump at 1,840 meters **relatively** quickly. After much searching, they discovered a pit—an area of a cave that falls straight down. Named "Millennium Pit," it allowed them to pass the 2,000-meter depth. More pits and passages led them to 2,080 meters, a spot they named "Game Over." But the caving game is never over. In 2009, Gennady Samokhin returned to Krubera. This time, he reached a depth of 2,191 meters. Then, in 2012, he broke his own record, diving to a point six meters deeper, at a total depth of 2,197 meters. And so the game goes on, with deeper and deeper caves calling out to be explored.

---

1 The **Caucasus Mountains** are in the country of Georgia, between the Black Sea and the Caspian Sea.

2 Something that is **inverted** is upside down.

3 A **ton** is a unit of weight equal to 2,000 pounds, or 909 kilograms.

4 A **cascade** is falling water.

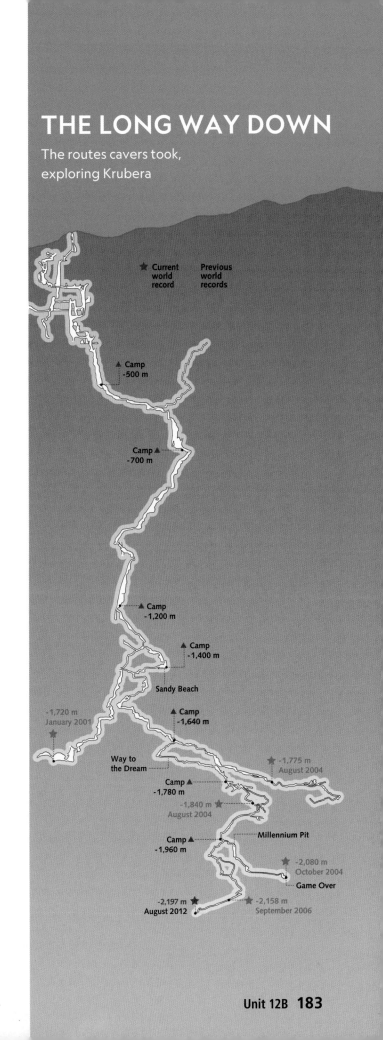

THE LONG WAY DOWN
The routes cavers took, exploring Krubera

★ Current world record   ★ Previous world records

Camp -500 m

Camp -700 m

Camp -1,200 m

Camp -1,400 m

Sandy Beach

-1,720 m January 2001

Camp -1,640 m

Way to the Dream

-1,775 m August 2004

Camp -1,780 m

-1,840 m August 2004

Millennium Pit

Camp -1,960 m

-2,080 m October 2004

Game Over

-2,197 m August 2012

-2,158 m September 2006

A. Choose the best answer for each question.

GIST

1. What is this passage mainly about?

    a. a cave near the South Pole

    b. a journey of cave exploration

    c. equipment needed for caving

DETAIL

2. How did the cavers solve the problem of the sump at 1,775 meters?

    a. They emptied it.

    b. They dove through it.

    c. They found a way around it.

REFERENCE

3. The word *it* in the third sentence of paragraph E refers to ___.

    a. the team

    b. the sump

    c. the passage

A caver emerges from Krubera Cave after a two-week expedition.

INFERENCE

4. Why was Samokhin smiling as he emerged from a test dive?

    a. He had discovered another sump.

    b. He had possibly found a way through the sump.

    c. He was happy that he was returning to the surface.

PURPOSE

5. What is the purpose of the last paragraph?

    a. to explain how a Ukrainian team rescued García-Dils's team

    b. to describe how excited the team felt when they finished their descent

    c. to explain that cavers will likely reach greater depths in the future

SCANNING

B. Scan the reading and match each person or group (a–c) with the sentence that describes them. Each person or group may be used more than once.

a. García-Dils's team	b. the Ukrainian team	c. Gennady Samokhin

1. ___ was the first to reach a depth of 1,775 meters.

2. ___ reached a depth of 2,191 meters.

3. ___ discovered and named the "Millennium Pit."

4. ___ discovered and named a spot called "Game Over."

5. ___ holds the world record for deepest descent.

6. ___ discovered and named a spot called "Way to the Dream."

Taking Notes on a Reading (3)—Creating a Visual Summary

For some reading passages, it can be helpful to organize your notes in the form of a diagram or sketch that relates to the overall topic of the passage. Doing so can help you engage with a text and present the information in a way that is clear to understand. The reading *Dark Descent* was about caving to extreme depths, so any notes could be organized as shown below.

SUMMARIZING **A.** Complete the notes using information from the reading passage and the infographic *The Long Way Down*.

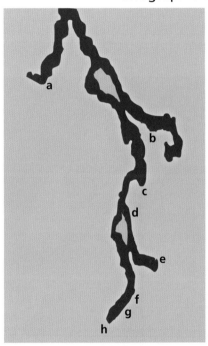

EXPLORING KRUBERA

a. **1,720 m**: Former world record for deepest point achieved by cavers; achieved in [1]_____

b. **1,775 m**: Reached by García-Dils's team in August 2004 but blocked by a [2]_____

c. **1,840 m**: García-Dils's team blocked again; found possible passage, but had low [3]_____, so had to return to surface

d. **2,000 m**: Depth passed by a team from Ukraine after finding the [4]_____

e. **2,080 m**: Area reached by Ukrainian team in October 2004 and named [5]_____

f. **2,158 m**: Reached in September 2006

g. **2,191 m**: [6]_____ reached here in 2009

h. **2,197 m**: Current record (as of 2019) held by Gennady Samokhin

SUMMARIZING **B.** Read the paragraph below about hang gliding records. Underline the references to years and distances. Then use this information to create a visual summary of the main points.

In 1994, hang gliding world champion Judy Leden set a new record for the highest altitude achieved in a hang glider. After being launched from a hot air balloon, Leden flew at an incredible height of 11,800 meters—a record that still stands today. In 1976, American Bob McCaffrey almost doubled the previous record when he flew at 9,631 meters. However, this height was bettered just two years later by French glider Stephane Dunoyer, who managed an altitude of 9,973 meters. In 1982, Canadian John Bird added 85 meters to the world record height. Bird held this record for 12 years until Leden's amazing flight.

DEFINITIONS **A.** Complete the definitions using the correct form of the words in the box.

block conquer necessity out of time supplies

1. Something that _____ your way stops you from moving forward.

2. A(n) _____ is something that you must have.

3. If you go camping, you need to take _____ like food and water.

4. When you _____ something, you overcome the challenges it presents.

5. When the bell rings and you haven't finished a test, you are _____.

COMPLETION **B.** Complete the information. Circle the correct options.

Cave expert Louise Hose had come to Oman to see if the country's caves could be made ¹**disappointed / relatively** safe, increasing the country's options for new tourist attractions. At the Well of Birds, a beautiful green pit with a ²**depth / block** of 210 meters, Hose used climbing ropes to ³**ease / emerge** her way down. Soon, she joined her group at the bottom, where they were ⁴**disappointed / eased** to discover that a black pool was ⁵**blocking / conquering** their way to the cave entrance. They swam to the other side, where they saw the water spill out of the pool and disappear into the cave system. After they ⁶**eased / emerged** from the water, they stopped to enjoy the natural beauty around them.

∧ **Louise Hose lowers herself into the Well of Birds.**

COLLOCATIONS **C.** The phrase *out of* can be used with many nouns, as in the phrase **out of time**. Complete the sentences using the words in the box.

choice gas necessity supplies

1. The car won't start because it's out of _____.

2. He works two jobs out of _____. Neither of them pays very well.

3. We're almost out of _____. There's only a little food and water left.

4. She still lives with her parents, but it's not out of _____. She can't afford her own place.

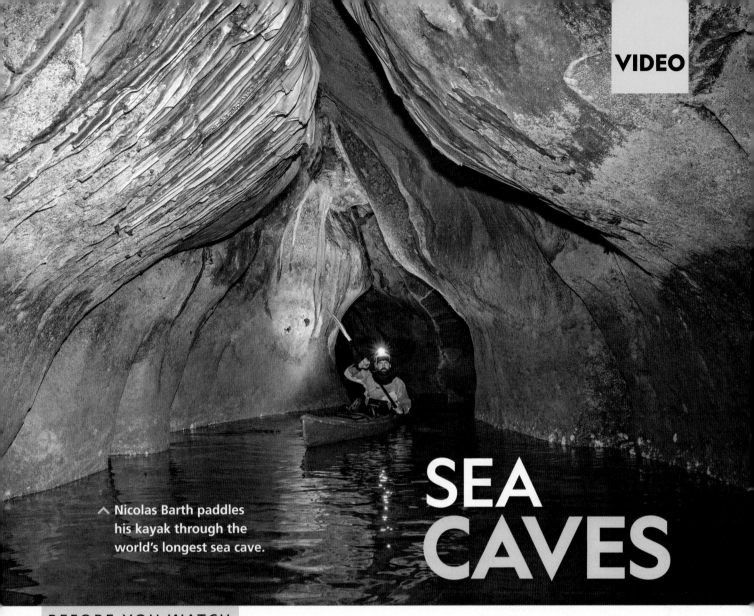

^ Nicolas Barth paddles his kayak through the world's longest sea cave.

SEA CAVES

BEFORE YOU WATCH

PREVIEWING **A.** Read the information. The words in **bold** appear in the video. Match each word with its definition.

In 2010, **geologist** Nicolas Barth was studying rocks on New Zealand's South Island. He decided to climb down a cliff and go for a swim, where—by chance—he came across a huge cave. Other people had seen Matainaka Cave before, but it wasn't until Barth and his team had explored and **surveyed** the cave system that it was revealed to be the longest in the world. Studying the cave was a huge task. Traveling by kayak, swimming, and sometimes crawling, Barth and his team moved slowly through the entire length of the system. "The cave passages can be as **narrow** as your body," explains Barth. "You might have to take your helmet off to be able to fit."

1. geologist • • a. a scientist who studies rocks

2. survey • • b. the opposite of *wide*

3. narrow • • c. to study a place, e.g., to create a map

DISCUSSION **B.** What do you think Barth and his colleagues learned from studying Matainaka Cave? Discuss with a partner and list some ideas.

WHILE YOU WATCH

GIST **A.** Watch the video. Which of your ideas in Before You Watch B are mentioned? What else did Barth and his team learn from studying the cave?

_____

_____

COMPLETION **B.** Watch the video again. Complete the notes about Matainaka Cave using the numbers in the box. One number is extra.

| 1.5 | 2 | 6 | 10 | 70 | 80 |

Matainaka Cave

- Longest sea cave in the world—around [1]____ kilometers
- [2]____% longer than any other sea cave
- Located in New Zealand, Otago Coast ([3]____ of the 10 longest sea caves are here)
- Around [4]____ thousand years old
- Each year, gets around [5]____ cm deeper

CRITICAL THINKING Synthesizing Information   Look back over the unit. What did each person below achieve? Whose achievement do you think is the most impressive? Note your ideas and reasons below. Then discuss with a partner.

| **Nicolas Barth** | **Judy Leden** | **Gennady Samokhin** | **Yves Rossy** |

_____

_____

_____

VOCABULARY REVIEW

Do you remember the meanings of these words? Check (✓) the ones you know. Look back at the unit and review any words you're not sure of.

Reading A

- ☐ cliff
- ☐ courage
- ☐ engine
- ☐ fantastic
- ☐ motivate*
- ☐ steer
- ☐ thrill
- ☐ tightly
- ☐ unlike
- ☐ wing

Reading B

- ☐ block
- ☐ conquer
- ☐ depth
- ☐ disappointed
- ☐ ease
- ☐ emerge*
- ☐ necessity
- ☐ out of time
- ☐ relatively
- ☐ supplies

* Academic Word List

Photo and Illustration Credits

Text Credits

Jan 2018, and "Arctic Sea Ice Is Second-Lowest on Record," by Craig Welch: news.nationalgeographic.com, **151** Adapted from "Last Ice," by Tim Folger: NGM, Jan 2018, **161** Adapted from "How Fake News Tricks Your Brain," by Alexandra E. Petri: news.nationalgeographic. com, **167** Adapted from "Why We Lie," by Yudhijit Bhattacharjee: NGM, June 2017, **175** Adapted from "If We Only Had Wings," by Nancy Shute: NGM, Sep 2011, **182** Adapted from "Call of the Abyss," by Alexander Klimchouk: NGM, May 2005

NGM = National Geographic Magazine

Acknowledgments

The Authors and Publisher would like to thank the following teaching professionals for their valuable feedback during the development of the series.

Akiko Hagiwara, Tokyo University of Pharmacy and Life Sciences; **Albert Lehner**, University of Fukui; **Alexander Cameron**, Kyushu Sangyo University; **Amira Traish**, University of Sharjah; **Andrés López**, Colégio José Max León; **Andrew Gallacher**, Kyushu Sangyo University; **Angelica Hernandez**, Liceo San Agustin; **Angus Painter**, Fukuoka University; **Anouchka Rachelson**, Miami Dade College; **Ari Hayakawa**, Aoyama Gakuin University; **Atsuko Otsuki**, Senshu University; **Ayako Hisatsune**, Kanazawa Institute of Technology; **Bogdan Pavliy**, Toyama University of International Studies; **Braden Chase**, The Braden Chase Company; **Brian J. Damm**, Kanda Institute of Foreign Languages; **Carol Friend**, Mercer County Community College; **Catherine Yu**, CNC Language School; **Chad Godfrey**, Saitama Medical University; **Cheng-hao Weng**, SMIC Private School; **Chisako Nakamura**, Ryukoku University; **Chiyo Myojin**, Kochi University of Technology; **Chris Valvona**, Okinawa Christian College; **Claire DeFord**, Olympic College; **Davi Sukses**, Sutomo 1; **David Farnell**, Fukuoka University; **David Johnson**, Kyushu Sangyo University; **Debbie Sou**, Kwong Tai Middle School; **Devin Ferreira**, University of Central Florida; **Eden Kaiser**, Framingham State University; **Ellie Park**, CNC Language School; **Elvis Bartra García**, Corporación Educativa Continental; **Emiko Yamada**, Westgate Corporation; **Eri Tamura**, Ishikawa Prefectural University; **Fadwa Sleiman**, University of Sharjah; **Frank Gutsche**, Tohoku University; **Frank Lin**, Guangzhou Tufu Culture; **Gavin Young**, Iwate University; **Gerry Landers**, GA Tech Language Institute; **Ghada Ahmed**, University of Bahrain; **Grace Choi**, Grace English School; **Greg Bevan**, Fukuoka University; **Gregg McNabb**, Shizuoka Institute of Science and Technology; **Helen Roland**, Miami Dade College; **Hiroshi Ohashi**, Kyushu University; **Hiroyo Yoshida**, Toyo University; **Hojin Song**, GloLink Education; **Jackie Bae**, Plato Language School; **Jade Wong**, Belilios Public School; **James McCarron**, Chiba University; **Jane Kirsch**, INTO George Mason University; **Jenay Seymore**, Hong Ik University; **John Appleby**, Kanda Institute of Foreign Languages; **John Nevara**, Kagoshima University; **Jonathan Bronson**, Approach International Student Center; **Joseph Zhou**, UUabc; **Junjun Zhou**, Menaul School; **Kaori Yamamoto**, **Katarina Zorkic**, Rosemead College; **Keiko Miyagawa**, Meiji University; **Kevin Tang**, Ritsumeikan Asia Pacific University; **Kieran Julian**, Kanda Institute of Foreign Languages; **Kim Kawashima**, Olympic College; **Kyle Kumataka**, Ritsumeikan Asia Pacific University; **Kyosuke Shimamura**, Kurume University; **Lance Stilp**, Ritsumeikan Asia Pacific University; **Li Zhaoli**, Weifang No.7 Middle School; **Liza Armstrong**, University of Missouri; **Lucas Pignolet**, Ritsumeikan Asia Pacific University; **Luke Harrington**, Chiba University; **M. Lee**, KCC; **Maiko Berger**, Ritsumeikan Asia Pacific University; **Mandy Kan**, CNEC Christian College; **Mari Nakamura**, English Square; **Masako Kikukawa**, Doshisha University; **Matthew Fraser**, Westgate Corporation; **Mayuko Matsunuma**, Seijo University; **Michiko Imai**, Aichi University; **Mei ho Chiu**, Soochow University; **Melissa Potts**, ELS Berkeley, **Monica Espinoza**, Torrance Adult School; **Ms. Manassara Riensumettharadol**, Kasetsart University; **My Uyen Tran**, Ho Chi Minh City University of Foreign Languages and Information Technology; **Narahiko Inoue**, Kyushu University; **Neil Witkin**, Kyushu Sangyo University; **Olesya Shatunova**, Kanagawa University; **Patricia Fiene**, Midwestern Career College; **Patricia Nation**, Miami Dade College; **Patrick John Johnston**, Ritsumeikan Asia Pacific University; **Paul Hansen**, Hokkaido University; **Paula Snyder**, University of Missouri-Columbia; **Reiko Kachi**, Aichi University / Chukyo University; **Robert Dykes**, Jin-ai University; **Rosanna Bird**, Approach International Student Center; **Ryo Takahira**, Kurume Fusetsu High School; **Samuel Taylor**, Kyushu Sangyo University; **Sandra Stein**, American University of Kuwait; **Sara Sulko**, University of Missouri; **Serena Lo**, Wong Shiu Chi Secondary School; **Shin Okada**, Osaka University; **Silvana Carlini**, Colégio Agostiniano Mendel; **Silvia Yafai**, ADVETI: Applied Tech High School; **Stella Millikan**, Fukuoka Women's University; **Summer Webb**, University of Colorado Boulder; **Susumu Hiramatsu**, Okayama University; **Suzanne Littlewood**, Zayed University; **Takako Kuwayama**, Kansai University; **Takashi Urabe**, Aoyama-Gakuin University; **Teo Kim**, OROMedu; **Tim Chambers**; **Toshiya Tanaka**, Kyushu University; **Trevor Holster**, Fukuoka University; **Wakako Takinami**, Tottori University; **Wayne Malcolm**, Fukui University of Technology; **Wendy Wish**, Valencia College; **Xingwu Chen**, Xueersi-TAL; **Yin Wang**, TAL Education Group; **Yohei Murayama**, Kagoshima University; **Yoko Sakurai**, Aichi University; **Yoko Sato**, Tokyo University of Agriculture and Technology; **Yoon-Ji Ahn**, Daks Education; **Yu-Lim Im**, Daks Education; **Yuriko Ueda**, Ryukoku University; **Yvonne Hodnett**, Australian College of Kuwait; **Yvonne Johnson**, UWCSEA Dover

GLOSSARY

These words are used in *Reading Explorer* to describe various reading and critical thinking skills.

Analyze   to study a text in detail, e.g., to identify key points, similarities, and differences

Apply   to think about how an idea might be useful in other ways, e.g., solutions to a problem

Classify   to arrange things in groups or categories, based on their characteristics

Evaluate   to examine different sides of an issue, e.g., reasons for and against something

Infer   to "read between the lines"—information the writer expresses indirectly

Interpret   to think about what a writer means by a certain phrase or expression

Justify   to give reasons for a personal opinion, belief, or decision

Rank   to put things in order based on criteria, e.g., size or importance

Reflect   to think deeply about what a writer is saying and how it compares with your own views

Relate   to consider how ideas in a text connect with your own personal experience

Scan   to look through a text to find particular words or information

Skim   to look at a text quickly to get an overall understanding of its main idea

Summarize to give a brief statement of the main points of a text

Synthesize to use information from more than one source to make a judgment or comparison

INDEX OF EXAM QUESTION TYPES

The activities in *Reading Explorer, Third Edition* provide comprehensive practice of several question types that feature in standardized tests such as TOEFL® and IELTS.

Common Question Types	IELTS	TOEFL®	Page(s)
Multiple choice (main idea, detail, reference, inference, vocabulary, paraphrasing)	✓	✓	10, 16, 26, 32, 42, 48, 57, 62, 72, 78, 88, 94, 104, 110, 119, 124, 133, 138, 147, 154, 163, 168, 178, 184
Completion (notes, diagram, chart)	✓		43, 48, 72, 89, 98, 105, 118, 142, 147, 154, 155
Completion (summary)	✓	✓	110, 114, 120, 125, 133, 138, 158, 188
Short answer	✓		10, 20, 33, 42, 78, 104, 124
Matching headings / information	✓		16, 26, 52, 94, 168, 169, 178
Categorizing (matching features)	✓	✓	57, 172, 184
True / False / Not Given	✓		32, 62, 66, 163
Rhetorical purpose		✓	16, 17, 57, 60, 72, 94, 104, 133, 154, 163, 184

The following tips will help you become a more successful reader.

1 Preview the text

Before you start reading a text, it's important to have some idea of the overall topic. Look at the title, photos, captions, and any maps or infographics. Skim the text quickly, and scan for any key words before reading in detail (see pages 11 and 33).

2 Use vocabulary strategies

Here are some strategies to use if you find a word or phrase you're not sure of:

- **Use context** to guess the meaning of new words (see page 58).
- **Look at word parts** (e.g., affixes) to work out what a word means (see page 79).
- **Look for definitions** of new words within the reading passage itself (see page 179).
- **Use a dictionary** if you need, but be careful to identify the correct definition (see page 164).

3 Take notes

Note-taking helps you identify the main ideas and details within a text. It also helps you stay focused while reading. Try different ways of organizing your notes, and decide on a method that best suits you (see pages 120 and 125).

4 Infer information

Not everything is stated directly within a text. Use your own knowledge, and clues in the text, to make your own inferences and "read between the lines" (see page 139).

5 Make connections

As you read, look for words that help you understand how different ideas connect. For example:

- words that show levels of **certainty** (see pages 49 and 134)
- words that explain **cause-and-effect** relationships (see page 89)
- words that describe **contrasting ideas** (see page 95)

6 Read critically

Ask yourself questions as you read a text. For example, if the author presents a point of view, is enough supporting evidence provided? Is the evidence reliable? Does the author give a balanced argument? (see pages 148 and 155)

7 Create a summary

Creating a summary is a great way to check your understanding of a text. It also makes it easier to remember the main points. You can summarize in different ways based on the type of text. For example:

- **timelines** (see page 43)
- **T-charts** (see page 89)
- **Venn diagrams** (see page 105)
- **concept maps** (see page 125)
- **research summaries** (see page 169)
- **visual summaries** (see page 185)